THE
SINGLE WOMAN'S
TRAVEL GUIDE

THE
SINGLE WOMAN'S
TRAVEL GUIDE

Jacqueline Simenauer
and Doris Walfield

CITADEL PRESS
Kensington Publishing Corp.
www.kensingtonbooks.com

CITADEL PRESS books are published by

Kensington Publishing Corp.
850 Third Avenue
New York, NY 10022

All Kensington titles, imprints, and distributed lines are available at special quantity discounts for bulk purchases for sales promotions, premiums, fund raising, educational, or institutional use. Special book excerpts or customized printings can also be created to fit specific needs. For details, write or phone the office of the Kensington special sales manager: Kensington Publishing Corp., 850 Third Avenue, New York, NY 10022, attn: Special Sales Department, phone 1-800-221-2647.

Citadel Press and the Citadel logo are trademarks of Kensington Publishing Corp.

First Citadel printing: September 2001

10 9 8 7 6 5 4 3 2 1

Printed in the United States of America

ISBN 0-8065-2156-2

Cataloging-in-Publication Information may be obtained from the Library of Congress.

For Peter and Tara, my lifelong traveling companions

For Tillie Himelstein, forever in my heart—J. S.

To my wonderful husband, Norman—all my love always. A special "I love you" for all your solitary dinners, doing the chores, and taking care of the dog while I was off enjoying my journeys as a solo woman traveler doing research for this book. You are the rock and joy of my life. And to my children, Brad, Lisa, Randi, and Heidi, for all the pleasure and encouragement you give me, I am truly blessed. Also, thank you to my sons-in-law John and Joel for the happiness you bring to our family. A special I love you to my grandkids, Talia, Jenna, Cara, Cody, and Kiley. You are the light of my life. May we all continue on life's journey together—D. W.

Contents

Introduction

*Nothing in the world is as powerful as an idea
whose time has come.*—Victor Hugo

This book is not like any other travel book! It does not rate
tours, hotels, restaurants, or cruise lines. Rather, this book is
all about making the solo woman's travel dreams come true. It is
exclusively dedicated to banishing any potential pitfalls, real or
imagined, you may encounter that could cloud your vacation. This
book enables you to venture forth and fulfill your travel dreams
at destinations near and far.

The Single Woman's Travel Guide is written for all women, of
every age, from all walks of life, who are excited by new experiences, meeting interesting people in must-see places, and leaving
the humdrum behind. Our goal is to energize every woman who
turns these pages into taking the journeys of her fantasies, whether
modest or monumental. Every woman can become a sophisticated,
world-wise traveler.

Not too long ago a woman we know lamented her certainty that
even though she had always wanted to go to Israel, she would
never get there. "Why not?" we asked. With a tone of astonish-
ment (as if to ask how we could even ask this question) she replied
that because her husband had passed away, she couldn't make the
trip. As her husband had been dead for over seven years, and she
was only in her early fifties, we again asked, "Why not?" Her

answer: "How could I go so far away without him?" Her manner of responding implied we were nuts to think of a woman making such a journey without a man at her side.

Alas, her plight is not uncommon. While scores of women are traveling to the far reaches of the world, too many others remain fearful of attempting to set out on their own. We know their doubts. There is concern about safety, making all the arrangements, feeling lonely, and the list of obstacles could continue well past the time they could have boarded the plane. Many women are waiting until a friend or relative can go with them. Others content themselves with getaways close to home or with taking the same vacation every year.

Too many women simply don't know about the many wonderful travel opportunities open to the solo woman traveler. Younger women with limited budgets are often unaware of all the affordable, attractive vacation offerings. Frequently travel agents don't know about or take the time to research vacations best suited to an individual woman's needs.

What a shame! The world in its infinite glory and beauty awaits discovery by each and every one of its inhabitants. An abundance of imaginative, affordable vacations makes these heady days for travelers. Today travel is the essence of fine living. Travel is a potent stress-reliever. And with 76 percent of us claiming that our stress levels are too high, travel is more important than ever. To miss out on the wonderment, pleasure, and knowledge that only travel can bring because of the simple reason of not wanting to go it alone is a costly mistake, just as it is to put off travel plans to some vague distant date or not to venture "too far." Travel keeps our minds alert and offers a new perspective on our world, our work, ourselves, and the people around us. Each day, month, year that you wait to make your traveling dreams a reality is time lost, never to be regained.

Both authors have traveled extensively, with and without companions. Yes, at times it is nice to have someone at your side, but there are bonuses to going it on your own. You are beholden to no one, you go and do as you please. And you're more tuned in to meeting others; you reach out more and give of yourself in a way that affords people a greater opportunity to respond to you. There is also a great sense of confidence gained from taking a trip solo. It goes far beyond the immediate gratification of the journey. You are your own person; you can go it alone and you know it. That's an exhilarating feeling!

In these pages you will find a trip for every travel taste. We have done all the hard work of researching everything the solo woman needs to know about traveling on her own. This runs the gamut from how to choose that special destination to how to secure the best airfares and how to make sure your travel agent is right for you. We even tell you how to stay safe, how to pack, and how to look your best without spending a lot of time doing it.

Tours Galore

Based on our extensive experience we believe the best, safest, most convenient, and most gratifying way for a woman on her own to enjoy any destination and any type of vacation is to take an escorted tour. Today, tours are happening in numerous exciting new venues to suit every taste. There are fantastic tours that cater to every age and preference. There are tours for those with a keen spirit of adventure, women-only tours, vacations for mothers or grandmothers who travel with children, and getaways for younger women who have romance on their mind, as well as tours for women "of a certain age."

One major advantage of tours is that they offer safety and security. What many (especially young) travelers don't realize is that traveling abroad is not as safe as they may believe. For some reason, many people think foreign places offer a measure of security not found in the United States—but this is not necessarily the case. It is especially inadvisable for young women to travel alone to countries where there are language barriers and cultural differences. For example, in many areas of countries such as Morocco, Turkey, and Egypt, it is frowned upon to wear shorts or sleeveless attire in public. Also, in some countries ordinary American friendliness can be misconstrued as flirting.

All tours have socializing built into them. Good friendships are often formed on tours. In fact, it's not uncommon for solo women with similar interests to meet on a tour and then become traveling buddies on later adventures. In these pages, you will learn about the ever-more-numerous different tours that are available including:

- *Special interest trips* that include everything from opera tours, cooking tours, and cultural/archaeological tours to vacations where you can indulge in your favorite craft. There are even religious trips to holy places and/or the land of your ancestors.
- *Athletic and adventure tours* that run the gamut from leisurely walking or pedaling a bicycle to riding the rapids or trekking in high mountains. There are vacations with close encounters with animals: You can swim with the dolphins, ride a camel or a horse, or take a helicopter to watch newborn baby seals. And if you're a space buff, believe it or not, there's even a vacation to let you experience weightlessness, and one coming up that will take you into outer space!
- *Spa holidays* pamper you and cater to your every whim and are great for relieving tension.
- *Women-only tours* are wonderful ways for gals to share a camaraderie with each other, as only women can, while venturing to the far corners of the earth.
- *Best-of-Europe itineraries* guides you through some of the continent's best-loved countries, showing you both modern and historic highlights.
- *Take-the-kids* vacations offer wonderful getaways moms (or grandmothers) and their children will enjoy. They are places with fun-filled activities for the pleasure of both generations.

The list of places to go and things to do goes on and on. There are frenzied-pace tours or slow, relaxing sojourns. There's something to fit every fancy and every pocketbook. Tour directors introduce you to the native culture, they point out all the important sights, they tell you the inside story at every bend. They take care of your needs and wants.

Because we are so impressed by the vast amount of irresistible tours available, we have devoted much of the book to information about them. These tours are scattered all over the world and they are especially innovative, intriguing, and incomparable learning experiences. Best of all, they're fun.

Cruises Galore

Cruising is another wonderful way for the solo woman to travel safely and not have to bother making arrangements. Cruising also automatically offers an easy way to meet other people. You not only get to know your tablemates, but every cruise offers activities that singles can participate in. Today's cruises go to the far reaches of the world. Some cater to fun in the sun, stopping at lands of gorgeous white sandy beaches and turquoise waters, while others send you to intellectually stimulating destinations where you can visit museums and spend time sight-seeing historic marvels. Moreover, there are cruises to fit all pocketbooks. Numerous cruise lines offer top-of-the-line luxury with gourmet food and astonishing nightclub acts. Still, for the budget-minded, there are cruises with more economical prices. And if you prefer singles-only cruises, there are those too.

We have gathered all the vital information necessary to make your vacation comfortable, convenient, affordable, enjoyable, and, most important, feasible. From choosing a destination, dealing with a travel agent, learning how to make your way around airlines, examining exciting and detailed itineraries around the globe, and looking your best on vacation to staying safe, these pages are brimming with everything you need to plan your dream trip.

We go into detail about the escorted tours we especially liked. We tell you a little about the tour operators and their philosophies, various destinations, and prices. We give you samples tours, complete with prices and a description of your likely companions. We tell you about the meals and accommodations included in the tour because, of course, one of the most enjoyable ways to explore other cultures is with a knife and fork and in the comforts of their lodgings. We tell you all about the cruise lines, what they have to offer, where they go, and the price.

The time to go is now! The selection of places to go has never been better! The choice is yours to make! Increasingly, single women are traveling to places they never dreamed of going to just a few short years ago. Moreover, women enjoy bonding with each other outside the workplace and they're doing it on the road. According to research conducted by NBC for a special segment on *The Today Show* about women who travel, 238 million women worldwide traveled without men in 1995. Women are spending more of their own discretionary income on travel.

With the millennium having just begun, make it your resolution to be the woman of the twenty-first century: Take to the open road and live your dreams. All you need to do is read on and have a great vacation!

PART I

PLANNING YOUR DREAM TRIP

Set yourself free! As the new century dawns, it foretells untold travel opportunities for you, the woman of the new millennium, throughout our wondrous planet. In bygone centuries, men were the explorers, the adventurers to seek new shores, to experience new cultures; now it is our turn!

But there's work to be done before you say your good-byes. A vacation is a very personal experience. What may be a dream holiday for one may be another's nightmare. It's up to you to make sure your vacation isn't a hit-or-miss affair. Those who choose well are sure to come home with more than just a fading tan and trinkets. A well-planned vacation can be a mind-body adventure that continues to bring a smile to your lips and your heart, lifting your spirits long after the experience has ended.

Of course, there is no question that many women take the same or similar vacation year after year, feeling that is the safest approach to a happy holiday. And yes, returning to the same place and doing the same exact things you did before requires no thought. It eliminates the research and planning. There is safety in knowing what to expect. But it also does away with the excitement and adventure of striking out in a new direction. Then too, through the years, our needs, likes, and desires change, sometimes so subtly we are not aware of them. What you enjoyed on your last vacation may not fit the bill right now.

Deciding where to go should be part of the fun of your vacation. Your first step in making your vacation dream a reality is selecting a destination. Don't regard it as a chore. Instead take your time, savor the planning, be sure the destination is right for you. Rave reviews from others mean little. We're all individuals with different needs and tastes.

1

Discovering Your Vacation Personality

The great men of antiquity judged that there was no better school for life than where one learns about the diversity of so many lives where one incessantly finds some new lesson in the great book of the world.—Montaigne 1580

Before hitting the open road alone, it's extremely important that you take time out to discover your vacation personality. Although traveling solo presents an ever increasing range of places and activities, what suits you best? What are your personal likes and dislikes away from home? Going alone can be the most wonderful present you ever give yourself if you take the time to make sure your holiday strictly suits your own taste, energy, budget, and timetable.

Take time to read and reflect on the questions that follow. Use your answers to determine what type of vacation is in your best interest at this time.

- Is there a destination you've always dreamed of going to? If so, what is standing in your way now? Does the reason for not going have real merit?

5

- Why are you taking this vacation and what do you hope to get out of it? Do you simply want to relax or are you looking for adventure and challenge?
- Are you an imaginative traveler? Are you seeking something more stimulating than swimming in a pool?
- Are you curious about discovering other cultures and meeting the local people?
- Are you drawn to nature and interested in wildlife?
- Do you prefer being a passive observer as opposed to being an active participant? Be honest—are you more of a couch potato?
- Are you self-sufficient, flexible, and able to accept situations as they exist? (This is a very necessary personality trait for women contemplating an action/adventure holiday.)
- What activities do you enjoy and what are your physical capabilities? While age has no barriers—some sixty-plus women can do things that many thirty-year-olds can't—only *you* can make that decision.
- Budget or deluxe? What kind of ambiance are you looking for? How much do you want to spend? Will you enjoy simple but comfortable accommodations or will you feel let down if your hotels are not five-star?
- Are you a history buff? Do you have a special fondness for witnessing places and things of the past?
- Is weather an important consideration? Do you fare best in a warm climate or can you face hardy weather conditions?
- Has your life seemed a little boring? Would you really appreciate some excitement and nightlife?
- Are you a shopping addict? Upon returning home from a holiday, do you feel let down if you don't have a lot of souvenirs?
- Do you have a need to enhance your general physical and mental well-being with a little pampering?
- Do you want to meet other women traveling alone?
- What form of transportation most appeals to you? Do you mind long trips?

Be honest with yourself. The answers to these questions will tell you what you really want out of a vacation. If, for example, you really aren't curious about exploring other cultures and are more of a couch potato who loves to relax by a pool, a luxurious spa may be just right for you. If you love to experiment with new recipes and would enjoy meeting other people with similar interests, then you might want to consider a special-interest vacation with cooking classes. If you have a fondness for the great outdoors and love animals, why not take one of the wonderful adventure vacations filled with outdoor activities?

Foremost, it's crucial to remember that this is *your* vacation! One advantage for the solo traveler is that you have no one to please but yourself. And why shouldn't you? You deserve it.

If you are straightforward in your answers you will have more than just a clue as to what type of vacation will best suit you now. Then begin to do more homework. Talk to friends and relatives who have been where you want to go. What do they recommend? Listen, but don't make any hasty decision based on what people tell you. Just file it away in your mind to be considered along with all your other information.

Next step: Consider one of the many trips in this book that fit your requirements. We have researched all the vacations we mention and know they are suitable and enjoyable for the solo woman traveler. Call for brochures. Read more about the destination. Does it still seem right for you? You have to take into account such variables as cost and length of program, but most important, concentrate on the itinerary and pace of the vacation. Does it address your requirements? If not, back up and take a look at another one of the tours mentioned. Or contact a reputable travel agent who will have your best interests at heart. Read our chapter on choosing a travel agent to determine who is the best one for you.

Be sure to give yourself plenty of time to decide. Make comparisons. When all is done, and you have made your choice, sit back, relax, and start looking forward to the vacation of a lifetime.

2

Unraveling the Airways Maze

If you are looking for perfect safety, you will do
well to sit on a fence and watch the birds; but,
if you really wish to learn to fly, you must mount
a machine and become acquainted with its tricks
and actual trials.—Wilbur Wright, 1901

Flying smart requires knowledge and effort. There's much to know about air transportation before you can breeze through it all. From deciding on a carrier to reaching your final stop and picking up your luggage at the baggage carousel, the entire flying experience can be daunting. Yet no woman needs to be intimidated by the complexities of traveling by air. All it takes is a little education to master this fast, efficient means of transportation that shrinks the globe, putting all destinations within your grasp.

Getting the Best Fare

The elimination of government regulation of the airlines has resulted in lower fares and a wide variety of prices. But you have to be a careful comparison shopper to get the best deal. The differences in air fares can be substantial. Here's where a good travel agent can be your first resource. Ask her to check all the airlines and their fares for your destination. Or, you can call the airlines direct and compare prices.

Be sure the travel agent is making inquiries about "consolidators" (agencies that buy tickets in bulk and thereby get better rates) and other sources of discounted seats that are not available directly from the airline. Bear in mind, however, that consolidator seats can have even more severe restrictions than the airlines' own deep-discount fares, particularly if the flight is delayed or canceled. Although consolidators have gotten a bad name, usually they are not shady deals, but you do have to watch out for the agents who may not be able to deliver what they promise. If you go this route, be sure you are dealing with a reputable travel agent, and that she has had experience with this consolidator. Read all the fine print, and pay by credit card. A good precaution is to check with a better business bureau to see if there are any complaints against the consolidator. Be sure you know exactly what you are getting for your money, what airline will you be going on, and what route. If a deal seems too good to be true, it probably is. Occasionally a travel agency will have a special deal with an airline for discounts. But you may have to ask; don't assume the agent will think of telling you.

The travel agent may also be able to get you a good deal on a public charter. These flights usually offer lower fares and often operate nonstop in markets where scheduled flights would be less direct. Also, many charters don't have all of the restrictions of scheduled-service discount fares, such as requiring that purchases be made way in advance or requiring a Saturday night stay-over. In addition, most charter flights aren't "capacity-controlled" like scheduled-service discount fares; every seat on the airplane is usually available at the advertised fare.

However, these charters do have restrictions that are spelled out in the contract. For example, the public charter operator or airline can cancel a flight for any reason up until ten days before departure. Your flight may be canceled if it doesn't sell well or for some other reason. During the last ten days before departure, a public charter can be canceled only if it is physically impossible to operate it. If you choose to go this route, be sure to carefully scrutinize the contract.

Always ask the travel or airline agent if your city of origin is an airline "hub." If so, fares may be higher than for flights from other nearby cities because of reduced competition. If you do live at a hub you might save money by leaving from another nearby city, even if you end up connecting through the hub where you live.

If you like scouring the Web, you can also check out sites that monitor fares. Some of them will search for the lowest fares. Sites include:

- www.economytravel.com
- www.cheaptickets.com
- www.lowestfare.com
- www.hotwire.com
- www.1800airfare.com
- www.priceline.com
- www.travelocity.com
- www.savvio.com
- www.onetravel.com
- www.bestfares.com
- www.webflyer.com
- www.expedia.com

If you are very flexible as to when you can take your holiday, a number of airlines send e-mail messages every week notifying subscribers of last-minute fare specials for departures within the next few days. See the airlines' Web sites for information about these programs, or call their reservations line. For a list of airline Web sites, go to http://www.airlines.com. Sometimes even airline reservations agents and travel agents are unaware of these fares.

When purchasing your ticket, whether directly from the airlines or through a travel agent, ask about cancellation or your ability to change the flight. Don't assume you will get a refund if you get sick. In fact, most discount tickets are now nonrefundable, but can be applied toward the purchase of another ticket with the same carrier. However, you usually have to pay an administrative charge and the difference between the fares for the old and new flights.

If you are a senior citizen the airline may offer you a discount. If you are a member of the airline's frequent-flyer program and are considering purchasing a promotional or deep-discount fare, ask if that fare will earn frequent-flyer miles.

A good idea is to pay for your ticket with a credit card. This will provide certain protections under federal credit regulations. For example, in the case of airline bankruptcies, passengers who charge their fare and are not provided service are able to have their credit card company credit their account for the amount of the fare.

Since fares change all the time, even after you have your ticket, you may want to call the airline or travel agent about a week before departure to confirm your reservations and check the fare. If the fare has gone down before your departure date, some airlines will refund the difference. But you have to ask.

Regardless of how you purchase your ticket, if you wish to get the lowest fare, you have to have some flexibility. Often the best deals may be limited to travel on certain days of the week (usually Tuesday through Thursday, or Friday night through Sunday morning) or particular hours of the day; for example, a late-night departure. Always ask the agent what is the lowest fare and what you need to do to qualify for it. If you are going during a holiday period, discount seats are usually "blacked out" during these times. However, you might be able to get a discount fare if you fly on the holiday itself; for example, New Year's Day.

Although planning ahead is a good rule of thumb, if you can bide your time you might be fortunate enough to encounter a fare sale. What happens is that many airlines put seats on sale for brief periods during the year. You might inquire of your travel agent or the airlines if they know of any sale coming up.

Always check fare information with all the airports that you have access to. If you live in a large metropolitan area with more than one airport, sometimes there can be a difference in the fare price depending on which airport you leave from. In addition, flights that make a stop along the way are sometimes cheaper than a non-stop flight.

Defensive Flying

When selecting a flight, be aware that a departure early in the day is less likely to be delayed than a later flight, due to "ripple" effects (planes being delayed throughout the day). If you book the last flight of the day, you could get stuck overnight.

When making a reservation, be sure the agent records the information accurately: the spelling of your name, the flight numbers and travel dates, and the cities you are traveling between. Be sure you know which airport you are leaving from if there is more than one in your area. It's important that the airline has both your home and work telephone numbers so they can advise you if there is a change in schedule.

On international flights, make certain your name is the same on your ticket and your passport. If your name has recently changed, bring documentation (e.g., a marriage certificate or court order). Your airline tickets are not transferrable: They cannot be sold or given to another person to use.

If possible, pick up your ticket from a travel agency or from one of the airline's airport or city ticket offices. The procedure for replacing a ticket lost in the mail can be difficult. Put your ticket in a secure place after you receive it and keep a separate record of the ticket number.

If you have a choice between two connections and the fares and service are equivalent, choose the one with the less-congested connecting airport to reduce the chance of misconnecting. In addition, consider potential unfavorable weather conditions when choosing a connecting city.

Ask about your exact routing. A "direct" (or "through") flight can have one or more stops. If you have a choice, select flights that minimize the potential for baggage going astray. Nonstop flights offer the least likelihood of a bag getting lost or misplaced. Your chances of this happening increase slightly with a direct or "through" flight (one or more stops, but no change of aircraft). It further increases with an on-line connection (change of aircraft but not airlines). Chances are even greater with an interline connection (change of aircraft and airline).

The day before your departure, call the airline to reconfirm your reservation. Flight schedules can change, and while you can expect the airline to call to notify you if this occurs, it's best to double-check. On international trips, most airlines require that you reconfirm your departure and return flights at least seventy-two hours before each flight. If you don't, your reservation may be canceled.

Treat your airline tickets as cash. If they are lost or stolen, it can be difficult to get replacements or a refund. Jot down the ticket numbers and carry the piece of paper it is written on separately from your ticket. If your ticket goes astray the airline will be able to process your refund application faster when you have this number, but still, a refund can take two to six months.

Report a lost ticket immediately to the issuing carrier. If anyone uses or cashes in your ticket while the refund is pending, the airline may refuse to give you your money back. In addition, there is a handling charge that the airline may deduct from the refund.

Be sure to check your ticket immediately after checking in for each flight on your trip. Airline agents may accidentally lift two coupons instead of one, and there goes your next flight.

Alternatively, you can avoid having to keep track of airline tickets altogether by going the route of electronic ticketing, (e-ticketing), whereby you don't receive paper tickets at all. Major airlines began electronic ticketing in 1994 to save on paper costs and labor. When you book your flight the airline gives you a con-firmation code and subsequently sends (or e-mails) you a receipt. When you get to the airport, if you wish to check in at the curb, simply show the attendant your receipt. If you do not have lug-gage you can go straight to your gate and check in there. While e-tickets can spare you the worry of losing tickets and avoiding long check-in lines, many air travelers feel at a disadvantage of not having paper tickets should bad weather force cancellation of flights and they want to change to another, because e-ticket holders must first get a paper ticket issued in order to change carriers. Also, when computers are down, paper tickets are hard-copy proof that a passenger is confirmed on a flight. The bottom line: For the most part, e-tickets are as reliable as their paper counterparts.

If you prefer a certain seat, get your seat assignment well in advance. This is more important than ever because the percentage of occupied seats on U.S. carriers is running at its highest level since 1940. Book your seat when you purchase your ticket. Usually, when about 65 percent of the seats on a flight have been assigned, the remainder will not be allocated until airport check-in. Airlines routinely oversell flights in anticipation of no-shows, and they don't want to issue more seat assignments than there are seats.

Check-in

One of the most important things you can do to make flying as agreeable and hassle-free as possible is to make sure you allow yourself plenty of time to arrive early at the airport and check in. Even if you already have a boarding pass and seat assignment, your seat may be given away if you do not arrive before the airline's deadline. If you don't like your assigned seat, hold your boarding pass until just before departure. Sometimes seats open up and you could be reassigned. If that doesn't work, board the carrier and watch for better seats that remain unclaimed. Once the aircraft closes its doors, go for that better spot.

Bring a photo ID to the airport. Airlines require this type of identification for security reasons. Make sure your name on the ticket is exactly as it appears on your identification. When you arrive at the airport, get a tag from the airlines to put on the outside of each one of your bags, even carry-ons, with your name and address, home and work telephone numbers. Put the same information inside each bag, with the addition of an address and telephone number where you can be reached at your destination. Look to see that the agent checking your bags attaches a destination tag to each one. Check to see that these tags show the three-letter code for your destination airport (ask the agent to tell you the code when purchasing your ticket). To avoid any confusion, remove tags from previous trips.

In case your checked luggage is delayed in reaching you, bring toiletries and a change of underwear in a carry-on bag. Checked baggage is subject to limits. On most domestic and international flights, it's two checked bags (three if you don't have any carry-on luggage). There may be an extra charge if you bring more or if you exceed the airline's limits on the size of the bags. On some flights between two foreign cities, your allowance may be based on the weight of the bags rather than the number of pieces. The same two bags that cost nothing to check at the beginning of your trip could result in expensive excess baggage charges in a city that has a weight system. If you are flying out of the country, ask the airline about the weight limit for every segment of your international trip, especially if you are changing carriers.

Don't overpack your bags. This puts pressure on latches, making it easier for them to pop open. Also, lock your bags. This may help to keep the latches from springing open.

Tips to Avoid Getting "Bumped"

Getting "bumped" is a very real concern, as airlines routinely overbook. The best way to avoid this problem is, once again, arrive at your check-in point early. If possible, be at the airline's check-in when it opens up. Each airline has check-in requirements and a check-in deadline. For domestic flights, the deadline varies from twenty minutes to an hour or more before the scheduled departure. Overseas destinations can require you to check in two to three hours before the scheduled departure. If you arrive late and make your flight, your luggage may not. If you miss the airline's check-in deadline, the carrier might not assume liability for your luggage if it is delayed or lost.

If you miss the ticketing or check-in deadline, you might lose not only your reservation but also your right to compensation if the flight is oversold. The last passengers to check in are the first to be bumped, even if they have met the carrier's deadline. If a flight is oversold (this is not illegal, and most airlines, as we already mentioned, overbook scheduled flights to compensate for no-shows), the Department of Transportation (DOT) requires airlines to ask for volunteers to give up their seats. These "bumped" passengers are entitled to compensation. But before you agree to this, ask these important questions:

- When is the next flight on which the airline can confirm your seat? If they offer to put you on a standby on another flight that's full, you could be stranded.
- Will the airline provide other amenities such as free meals, a hotel room, phone calls, or ground transportation? If not, you will be responsible for these expenses while waiting for your next flight.

The DOT does not require the airlines to give volunteers who are bumped a specific sum. You may negotiate with the airline for a mutually acceptable amount of money or a free trip. Airline employees have guidelines for bargaining with passengers. If the airlines offer you a free ticket, ask about restrictions. How long is the ticket good for? Is it "blacked out" during periods you may want to use it? Can it be used for domestic and international flights? Most important, can you make a reservation, and if so, how far before departures are you permitted to make it?

If you are involuntarily bumped, DOT does require the airline to give you a written statement describing your rights and explaining how the carrier decides who gets on an oversold flight and who doesn't. Frequently, travelers who don't get to board their intended flight are entitled to an on-the-spot payment of denied boarding compensation. The amount depends on the price of the ticket and the length of the delay. However, if you are bumped involuntarily and the airline arranges substitute transportation that is scheduled to get you to your final destination within one hour of your original arrival time, there is no compensation.

On the other hand, if the airline arranges substitute transportation that is scheduled to arrive at your destination between one and two hours after your original arrival time (between one and four hours on international flights), the airline must pay you an amount equal to your one-way fare to your final destination, with a $200 maximum. If the substitute transportation is scheduled to get you to your destination more than two hours later (four hours internationally), or if the airline does not make any substitute travel arrangements for you, the compensation doubles (200 percent of your fare, $400 maximum).

You always get to keep your original ticket and use it on another flight. If you choose to make your own arrangements, you can request an "involuntary refund" for the ticket for the flight you were bumped from. The denied boarding compensation is essentially a payment for your inconvenience.

Baggage Safety

Most luggage looks alike, and that means it can be difficult to pick your luggage out of the assortment on the baggage carousel. You may want to put a colored label on your suitcase for quicker identification. After pulling a bag from the carousel, don't just assume it is yours: make a quick check of the name tag to ensure it is yours.

If a bag is opened or damaged, see if any of the contents are missing or damaged. Report any problems to the airline before leaving the airport. Open your suitcase as soon as you reach your destination. Any pilferage or damage should be immediately reported to the airline. Make a note of the date, time of call, and the person you spoke with. Follow up with a certified letter to the airline. Don't panic if a suitcase does not arrive. Airlines have sophisticated systems for tracking down luggage, and misplaced baggage is usually returned within hours. In many cases the airline will absorb any reasonable expenses you incur while they look for your missing bag. However, you and the airline will have to negotiate this sum, as you each may have different ideas as to what is reasonable. Always pack valuables in a carry-on.

Tips to Avoid Jet Lag

One of the major annoyances of flying long distances is crossing time zones, resulting in the curse of modern air transportation— we call it jet lag. Symptoms include insomnia or sleepiness, fatigue, lack of energy, even digestive problems and moodiness that can last for a day or a couple of days. What's more, recovery can be uneven—you feel good one day and bad the next. But there are simple ways to avoid the problem as follows:

- Get plenty of sleep before the day you are to board the plane. Plan to have all your packing and last-minute chores completed well before the time of takeoff.
- Don't drink alcohol during your flight. Alcohol may make you temporarily sleepy during the trip, but it won't give you a normal sleep. Alcohol also contributes to dehydration. Instead drink lots of water, club soda, or juices.

- Sleep during the flight (not during descent). Don't get up for dinner or the movie.
- During the flight, do isometric exercises.
- If you do eat during the flight, eat light.

Air travel is by far the fastest mode of transportation, and it can also be the most enjoyable now that you have learned all about how to be a sophisticated air passenger. Best of all, you can look forward to more and more trips to all sorts of interesting and exotic destinations. So board your flight, sit down, relax, and marvel at the technology that allows you to soar like a bird.

3

All Travel Agents Are
Not Created Equal

*I have but one lamp by which my feet are guided,
and that is the lamp of experience.*—Patrick Henry

All travel agents are not created equal. Don't automatically assume that because a travel agent is conveniently located in your neighborhood, this is the one you should use. The fact is, travel agents differ in knowledge and what they are willing to do for you. Choose a travel agent with care.

But, first of all, the question arises: Do you need a travel agent? This really is up to each individual and depends on the type of vacation you're considering. This book gives you in-depth information about many types of getaways that require no more of you than simply calling the 800 number provided. And those of you who feel comfortable dealing with airlines directly may just need to spend some time and have a little patience to contact destinations and make reservations yourself.

There may be more to your vacation than just deciding on a carrier and hotels. For example, are you interested in tours and package deals (land and air) for one price, and getting the best deal? Do you wish to put together your own itinerary? The more complicated the trip, the more time it will take you to put it together, and a travel agent can be a good resource.

However, if you decide you require the services of a travel agent to help you with your vacation plans, be careful in making your choice. Think of it like this: The travel agent is the first person you encounter who can have a profound impact on your vacation pocketbook and pleasure quotient. She may be your first line of defense against making a costly mistake, emotionally or financially.

What immediately comes to mind is a scene witnessed on a cruise taken by one of the authors of this book. As passengers were boarding the cruise ship, a distraught woman was standing on the pier arguing with ship personnel, who told her she could not board because her name was not on the roster. She kept trying to tell them this was an error. She had her ticket, but that didn't seem to matter. Eventually, she called her travel agent, who said she had no idea why her name was not on the ship's list of passengers but told her to call back in thirty minutes. During that time, we later learned, the travel agent called the ship's regional office to straighten out the mess. She insisted that the office call the ship and let her client board. In the end, the frustrated woman was allowed to embark, thanks to the fast action of her travel agent. She later told us that she always used this agent and had complete confidence in her.

Of course, this story might not have had the happy ending it did. We've all heard vacation horror stories, and a travel agent can be your first protection against a vacation going sour.

You need to exercise the same care in selecting a travel agent as you would any important person in your life. Therefore, just as you would ask friends and relatives to recommend a doctor, lawyer, or dentist, ask them about their dealings with travel agents. Ask your business associates and colleagues for a recommendation. A referral also tells the travel agent that you are serious and not just a shopper. This helps to ensure that the travel agent will make a greater effort for you.

When you do visit a travel agency, look around the office. Is it neat and tidy? Are there multitudes of travel brochures and are they efficiently arranged? Do you feel a sense of confidence about the agent who is assigned to you? You don't want to entrust your travel plans and your money to someone who looks disorganized and unprofessional.

Don't be timid about asking a lot of questions about the travel agent's background and knowledge. Your first question may be whether the agent is going to charge you a fee. If she is, the fee schedule should be provided right up front. In the past, you could expect that the travel agent who assisted you would be paid a commission by the airlines, hotels, and travel companies. But more recently, travel agencies have begun to tack on a fee.

It all started in September 1997, when the airlines cut back the commission they paid to travel agents. According to the American Association of Travel Agents (ASTA), the level of compensation that travel agents now get from the airlines has gone below what it costs them to process a ticket. ASTA is the world's largest travel trade association, primarily composed of travel agents and suppliers (airlines, car rentals, cruise lines). It has only been since 1998 that the majority of agents have been implementing service fees all across the board, but typically it is a nominal fee. It may cost you $5 to $20 to get a ticket. But usually, ASTA says, it is more than worth it because you save money in the long run by using the agent. Private research from organizations, like television's *20/20*, have shown that if you get a ticket from an airline directly it may cost more than it would if purchased through a travel agent. The reason for this is that usually the agent will research the various fares available from all the carriers going to your destination and select the cheapest one.

If you are looking to book a cruise or just hotels, you may be hit with a consultation fee that, if you ultimately make the purchase, the agent will apply to the total cost of your trip. If you come in and simply utilize the agent's time for a couple of hours and you don't buy anything, then you might be paying a fee that could be in the $50 range.

Ask if the agency is a member of ASTA; most reputable travel agencies are. ASTA's goal is to enhance the professionalism of member agents through effective training and meeting the needs of the traveling public. Members must abide by ASTA's code of ethics, which include the following:

- *Accuracy*—Members will be factual and accurate when providing information about their services and the services of any firm they represent. They will not use deceptive practices.
- *Disclosure*—Members will provide in writing, upon written request, complete details about the cost, restrictions, and other terms and conditions of any travel service sold, including cancellation and service fee policies.
- *Responsiveness*—Members will promptly respond to their client's complaints.
- *Refunds*—Members will remit any undisputed funds under their control within the specified time limit. Reasons for delay in providing funds will be given to the claimant promptly.
- *Conflict of Interest*—Members will not allow any preferred relationship with a supplier to interfere with the interests of their clients.
- *Cooperation*—Members will cooperate with any inquiry conducted by ASTA to resolve any dispute involving consumers or another member.

You may also ask if the travel agent has been certified by the Institute of Certified Travel Agents (ICTA), which offers travel agents curricula of rigorous courses pertaining to the travel industry. An agent who has completed the program shows that she has gone the extra mile in educating herself in the travel industry. This is a person who cares enough to take extra courses and do extra work to achieve certification. Agents can acquire two levels of certification. The first is the Certified Travel Associate (CTA) designation; this is given to people with a minimum of eighteen months' experience in the travel industry, and who have passed the CTA certification exam. The next level of certification is the Certified

Travel Counselor (CTC); this requires the agent to have a minimum of five years' travel industry experience and to have successfully completed a total of twelve courses set up by the ICTA.

You might also want to find a travel agent who specializes in your destination or the kind of vacation you are interested in. Today specialization is the order of the day in the travel industry. Some agents are even "certified" as specialists in a specific destination. These agents have to go through a training program that is usually provided by the tourist board of that particular destination to obtain their certification. For example, there is a Caribbean tour organization that comprises all the various Caribbean destinations and that has its own certification program. This type of program allows agents to significantly expand their knowledge of a particular destination and get certified for it.

The best way to find an agent who specializes in where or what you are interested in is to call the American Society of Travel Agents (ASTA) at 1-800-965-ASTA (2782). Or you can access the same information through their Web site, www.ASTANET.com.

Always ask the agent if she has been where you want to go. Of course, every agent's specific level of information is going to differ. There are some who have traveled extensively on a regular basis to some of the destinations they are selling. Such a person understands the destination and will, hopefully, be able to provide you with extra details and knowledge that you might otherwise not be able to get from brochures that, of course, are not interactive.

At the same time, be aware of the agent's questions and attitude toward you. Does she seem genuinely interested in fulfilling your needs or is she trying to sell you something you really are not interested in? Keep in mind the fact that a travel agent, while not working for a particular tour operator, may get a higher commission from one than another. Or he may get other incentives from a preferred company. Be alert and notice if an agent is steering you away from something you are particularly interested in and toward some other deal that may be more beneficial to the agent than to you. If an agent is real pushy and seems determined to sell you something, don't hesitate to ask why she is so intent on that particular deal. Always remember, this is your vacation; advice is fine, but you must make the final decisions. Today most travel agents understand that if you are not a satisfied customer you will not be coming back. If she steers you wrong once, that's it for her. And repeat business is what keeps travel agents in business.

On the other hand, you have to work with the agent. Let her understand your needs and concerns, what you like and don't like. Do you prefer a lot of sight-seeing and shopping? Do you want to join a group? How flexible are you in your travel arrangements? For example, if you live near more than one airport, do you care which airport you use, or is it a matter of obtaining the cheaper ticket? Remember, if you have to leave your car in the airport parking lot you may be using up the money saved on the lower fare. Do you have a specific time frame? Can you deviate from it in any way? What is your travel budget? If you have had a bad experience on a previous getaway, talk about that so you can avoid the same thing happening again. An agent is only as good as the information she gets from her client as well as the travel supplier.

To a woman traveling solo, safety is an important issue. Ask the agent if she has any knowledge about the location of the hotel you will be staying at and the relative safety of that area. Are there any places that should be avoided at this destination?

If you really hate eating alone, ask if the hotel provides room service. You might also want to ask what kind of health and fitness facilities are available, if not in the hotel, then in the immediate vicinity. If you are planning on taking a tour , question the agent about it. What is included and not included? What meals are included and what is the quality of the meals? Ask about the hotels and their locations, whether you can check in upon an early-morning arrival after a transatlantic flight. Ask about penalties for canceling. Finally, if you do not feel completely comfortable that the agent is working in your best interests, walk out the door and find someone who will.

Once you have a satisfactory experience with a travel agent, it's a good idea to have her assist you in setting up your next trip. The more the agent gets to know you and your needs, the easier it will become for both of you to get the best possible deals on future vacations. A travel agent can be the hand that guides you into making the best possible vacation decision. It's worth the effort to find one who will work hard in your best interest.

4

Tips on Safety, Money, Health, and More

A journey is a person in itself; no two are alike. And all plans, safeguards, policies, and coercion are fruitless. We find after years of struggle that we do not take a trip; a trip takes us.—John Steinbeck

After reading the above quotation, an immediate thought comes to mind: If all safeguards are fruitless, why bother being self-protective and prudent while on vacation? Why not just say: *"Que sera, sera,* whatever will be, will be"? And if that is not the case, then Steinbeck's quote doesn't hold water. What it all boils down to is this: as Steinbeck says, no two trips are alike, and the trip that is perfect is rare.

There is always an element of the unknown when you venture out. What all savvy trekkers learn from the vicissitudes of travel is that to enjoy a vacation, there are three rules to follow: Be flexible about some things, be stubborn about others, and know when to go with which. Your attitude can make or break your holiday. If our many years of travel have taught us anything, it is that there are always variables (big and little) beyond our control. Flights may not be on time, weather is unpredictable, machines from a tour bus to a blow-dryer can break down, new foods can give you a tummy ache, the person sitting next to you may talk too much, you may have forgotten to pack your best dress or left your walking shoes home—the list goes on and on.

Most journeys do go pretty much as planned. Vacation planners and managers work hard to ensure that you get what you pay for and more. And if you give time and thought to your vacation, most likely it will fulfill your fantasy. But it's important to be flexible and willing to accept the little problems that arise as just being part of the adventure. Be flexible in your expectations. For example, weather changes are often part of the adventure. A day's cruise or a flight to another destination on your itinerary may be canceled or delayed due to inclement weather. In most cases, your tour guide will be prepared for such occurrences. Often plan B is just as good as the original plan. We remember one incident where we were looking forward to a cruise on the Thames River in London, but heavy rains kept us on dry land. That afternoon our guide took us to the world-renowned Harrods department store and then to a charming café for tea. We all had a wonderful time.

Be lighthearted about unexpected situations, even if they are a bit disappointing. For example, a tour bus may be delayed by traffic or unforeseen roadwork and you may miss a scheduled visit. Take a minute to close your eyes and breathe slowly. Let the tension drain away. Make a deliberate effort to quickly get past the disappointment.

Tolerance toward others, especially tour members, will be appreciated. Remember, your relaxed state of mind will rub off on everyone else. For example, both authors have had the experience of getting off schedule because a tour member was late getting on the bus. Sometimes, people oversleep in the morning or become so engrossed in their own activities that they don't get back to the motorcoach at the time given by the tour leader. You have to make a concentrated effort to accept that once something goes wrong and passes it's best to forget it.

The rule *be forceful* applies to making sure you stay safe and avoid mishaps on your journey. These are aspects of travel that are largely in your control. A very real concern in our world is that of safety. The good news is that you're safer on vacation than you are at home, according to recent surveys by the U.S. Dept. of Justice and the Travel Industry of America. Crimes against travelers occur 40 percent less often than crimes against nontravelers thanks to increased security efforts by host areas and travelers themselves. Still, it's wise to take precautions throughout your trip. Unfortunately, wherever you are in the world, there are some people who will abuse the confidence of tourists and take advantage of an occasional lack of alertness. So that you may avoid any hassles, it's a good idea to observe certain guidelines. While some people may say you're paranoid if you pay too much attention to safety, remember: better safe than sorry. Here are some safeguards we have gathered over our years of travel.

Hotel Safety

To avoid theft, hotels have implemented magnetic-strip card keys, double locks, and peepholes. But it is still incumbent upon you to take steps to avoid thievery. To stay safe, follow these rules:

- Stay at a reputable hotel, preferably a branch of an international chain. Avoid cheap hotels (In China and Thailand they often double as brothels).
- Do not leave your bags, suitcases, or any other type of belongings unattended while checking in or out.
- Request that your room not be on the first two floors: This is where most thefts take place. Ask for a room on the fourth or fifth floor—high enough to discourage intruders and low enough to be easily reachable by firefighters.
- Ask for a room not too far from the elevator where people are constantly going back and forth. The safest rooms are those clearly visible from the elevator.
- If possible, obtain a room that opens into an interior hallway, not to the outdoors.
- Upon entering your room, immediately check all windows and doors for proper locking mechanisms. If the room has a

sliding glass door, check that it is closed every time you enter your room as the cleaning staff may sometimes open it and forget to lock it. Also check closets, shower stalls, and under the bed.

- After checking into your room, walk down the hallway and count the number of doorways to the closest exit. This can save your life in an emergency. (It's also a good idea to do this in an airplane).

- If something doesn't "feel right," do not hesitate to call the hotel security and discuss it with them. That's what they're there for.

- Never open your door to someone you don't know. If the person claims to be a member of the hotel staff, call the front desk to check if this true and find out why that person is there.

- If something goes wrong in your room and you feel uncomfortable with a male employee attending to it while you're in the room, ask for a member of the hotel security staff to be present or a female receptionist to be present.

- Never feel foolish about anything having to do with your sense of security regarding safety.

- If you feel insecure about entering an elevator alone with a strange man, wait for the next elevator or have a member of the hotel security staff accompany you.

- If you feel uneasy about a person in the lobby watching you enter an elevator, press a number of different buttons so that person doesn't know where you got off.

- When you go out for an evening, leave a light and the TV on, and hang the DO NOT DISTURB sign outside. It's best not to let people passing by know you are not in your room.

- Close the windows and the door whenever you leave your room—even if it's just to go next door or down the hall to a vending machine.

- Do not leave your key on the reception counter; always hand it over to a receptionist or drop it in the key slot at reception.

- Never leave the PLEASE MAKE UP MY ROOM sign out. This is an announcement that you are not in the room. The maid has a list of rooms to clean and she will get to your room sooner or later.
- Make sure you put the chain on your door at night. If the room does not have a chain, place a chair under the doorknob.
- Ask the tour director for his or her room number in case of an emergency.

Protecting Your Valuables

- Use the hotel safe, or the safe provided in your room to hold anything of value, including cash and your airline tickets. Find out whether the hotel is responsible if the safe is robbed. In some cases, hotels say they are not responsible for the safe in your room, but they are for the front-office safe.
- Leave your expensive jewelry at home. Never wear eye-catching jewelry where it can easily be seen. Do not take anything (keys, photos, etc.) with you that will create an emotional or financial hardship if lost or stolen.
- Take with you only the credit cards you intend to use. It's a good idea to bring at least one internationally recognized credit card. Make sure you have enough credit on the card to carry you through your journey.
- If you take jewelry, cameras, furs, and other new items that were made outside the United States and Canada and were imported, be sure to register these at customs before you leave. It takes only a minute or so and eliminates a potential argument when you return. You may register articles at any customs office, including those at airports, at no charge.
- Carry your passport at all times. It is one of your most important possessions when you are out of the United States. Before you leave home, make three photocopies of your passport: Leave one at home and tell someone where it is; keep one in your luggage (away from your original passport); and

leave one in the hotel safe. If your passport is stolen or lost, these precautions can save you a lot of time and aggravation when trying to get a new passport issued in a foreign country.

- When swimming or snorkeling place your passport and other valuables in a large envelope, seal it, and check it with the hotel's reception with instructions that it be put into their safe until you return. If you are not in the vicinity of your hotel and you're with a tour, ask the tour director if he or she has a locked secure place on the motor coach to leave these items. Again, keep these in a closed envelope.

- Bring most of your money in traveler's checks. You may want to take your traveler's checks in larger denominations as banks usually have a fixed-rate service charge. Usually it's best to take a little bit more than you think you need rather than worry about any unforeseen expenses or purchases. You can always cash in unused traveler's checks at the end of your vacation. Make two lists of the traveler's check numbers; keep one separate from the actual checks, and leave the other at home (again, tell someone you trust where it is). Never countersign a traveler's check until the moment you use it. Convert the checks to local currency as needed. Keep only enough cash on hand for a day or two. Many countries have ATMs that can be accessed by your local bank card. Inquire about this before your departure. Check with your bank to ensure you can withdraw cash on your card if necessary.

Street Safety

- Never tell someone you meet outside of your immediate group that you are traveling alone. Always say you're with friends or a tour group.

- Take a piece of hotel stationery with its address and telephone number with you before going out. If you should lose your way, go into a store and show a clerk the hotel's letterhead, and ask how you can get back. This is often safer than asking someone on the street.

- Be leery of friendly male strangers. Women traveling alone often are assumed to be looking for male companionship, someone to share their cash with. Don't be fooled by sweet talk. Your replacement is arriving with the next group of tourists.
- Avoid eye contact with strangers, especially men. In many foreign cultures, ordinary American friendliness is interpreted as provocative.
- Make sure you read a street map before venturing out on your own in a new town or city. If you are going to a specific destination or area, ask the tour guide or the concierge in your hotel for directions. Study them before you leave so you have a good idea of where you're going. Refer to them occasionally when out but don't pause to study them. Walk the streets like a native and try not to stop on street corners while you get deeply absorbed in reading your map. If you truly need to concentrate on your map while out, do it in the restroom stall of a hotel or restaurant.
- Always walk with confidence, head up and shoulders back.
- If you are walking by yourself in an area where English is not spoken, carry a metal whistle around your neck. If you feel uncomfortable with someone who has approached you, don't hesitate to blow it loudly.
- Don't dress outrageously.
- In the street, underground, tram, train, bus, or taxi, keep your handbag closed, hold on to it, and keep an eye on it all the time.
- Do not change money on the street.
- If you are drawing money by credit card from ATM, be circumspect.
- Don't place any valuables in outer pockets.

Tips to Avoid Overpaying

As a U.S. resident, you are paying tax in Europe that you don't owe. Up to 24 percent of the purchase price of nearly everything you buy contains a hidden Value Added Tax (VAT). Be a savvy shopper and learn how to get the tax refunds you deserve. First, shop where you see the GLOBAL REFUND TAX FREE SHOPPING sign. When you make a purchase, ask for the Global Refund Cheque. Some stories will only give you this when your purchase adds up to a certain amount. You have to ask before you buy. When leaving a country you have to show your purchases (don't pack your VAT-taxed goods before you return home; some countries will not refund VAT on items not in their original, sealed packages) and your Global Refund Cheques to customs and get them validated. You will receive your cash refund by cashing your Global Refund Cheques at the Cash Refund Office after you have cleared passport control or at any one of the Cash Refund Offices worldwide. Alternatively, you can mail your validated Global Refund Cheques to them and your credit card account will automatically be credited.

- When taking a cab, select one that has the emblem of a taxi company on the door. If you know in advance you are taking a cab from one place to another, ask your tour director or the hotel concierge about how much it should cost.
- When entering a cab, make sure the meter has not been running before you got in. Ask the driver approximately how much the ride will cost. If you think it is too much, say so or leave the cab. Always ask for a receipt.
- When paying in a restaurant, see if the tip has already been added to the bill.
- Bargaining is common in many outdoor shopping markets. It never hurts to ask for a better price.

Before You Go

- Try to exercise regularly at least two months before your trip. Make sure you are in the best possible condition. Being physically fit heightens your experience.

- Visit your doctor and dentist. Don't chance having a toothache or some other preventable problem on your vacation. According to a recent travel sickness survey, sponsored by Novartis Consumer Health (makers of Transderm Scop, a skin patch by prescription to avoid motion sickness), the most common sickness complaints among travelers were: sunburn (63 percent), motion sickness (35 percent), allergies (34 percent), traveler's diarrhea (24 percent), and food poisoning (12 percent).
- Get a manicure and pedicure before you leave home. It's usually best to wear a light color that won't look so bad when chipped.
- If you are planning on having a facial before you go, do it a week or so before in order to avoid any redness during the trip.
- Don't experiment with a new haircut just before you go. Do it about one month before your departure date. It's best to go with a style you know how to work with. You don't want to have to spend extra time fiddling with your hair.

Packing

- Make sure you have a secure place for all your traveling documents (passport and visa, if required, airline tickets with photo ID, traveler's checks, tour confirmation, hotel reservations, etc.) Always carry these with you when traveling from one destination to another.
- Always travel with small-size beauty products, lotions, and other toiletries. Without exception it's in your best interest to travel with as few possessions as possible, and that includes cumbersome beauty aids. Otherwise, packing and unpacking during your trip can become a hassle. And, of course, you want to leave as much room in your suitcase for goodies garnered in shopping expeditions.
- Purchase small plastic containers used for medications from your pharmacy. Fill these with everything from body lotion

and shampoo to vitamins and liquid laundry soap. Label accordingly. Place all containers with liquid contents in a Ziplock plastic bag so that if one accidentally opens, it will not mess up your other possessions. Avoid pressure-can type products that can burst in a depressurized aircraft.

- If you use a high-voltage blow-dryer, you may want to purchase a travel-size dryer. Many hotel bathrooms abroad have them, but they are not very powerful. However, overseas it is usual to find 220-volt, 50-cycle alternating current. Therefore, you must use an adapter/converter or the heavier voltage will instantly burn out the appliance. If you take a hair dryer, shaver, or iron, you will need an adapter (so the prong plug will connect to the various electrical supply outlets in different countries) and a converter (to convert the 220 volts to 110 volts). Adapter/converter kits that include the entire range of plugs can often be found in electrical supply stores and stores such as Wal-Mart.
- Travel light. A good rule of thumb is *if in doubt, leave it out.*
- Bring mix-and-match clothing to avoid taking too much and things you'll probably never wear. The best way to do this is to settle on a color theme before you go. Wrinkle-resistant, easy-care cotton and polyester clothing is often your best bet for touring. If your itinerary calls for evenings out, bring one dress-up outfit, perhaps a long black skirt with one or two different tops to match, and some dressy costume jewelry (leave the good stuff home).
- Find out what the climate is likely to be at the destination so that you can bring the appropriate garments. But be prepared for the unexpected. Bring a folding umbrella, a sweater, and a raincoat (with removable liner for spring and fall). Plan some outfits with layering in mind. It may be colder or warmer than normal and you may be traveling through different climates and altitudes.
- Never leave home without a comfortable pair of walking shoes. Achy feet will make you irritable. Also, bring one pair

of dress shoes, lightweight folding slippers, and sandals if you are going to be in warmer climates, as well as beach thongs or pool shoes.

- Check that you've included a toothbrush, toothpaste, deodorant, razor and shaving cream (if necessary), sunscreen, eye makeup remover, cleanser, sun hat (for sunny climates), plenty of small packages of tissues, two washcloths (some foreign hotels don't supply them), and a plastic bag for damp laundry.

- Bring an ample supply of any medications you are taking, copies of prescriptions, and the telephone and fax numbers of your doctor. If you wear eyeglasses, bring an extra pair. If you wear contact lenses, pack eyedrops and use them frequently if you are traveling in a dry climate. Carry medicines in your hand luggage.

- Bring aspirin or a similar over-the-counter type medication, Band-Aids, diarrhea medication, and a small pair of scissors, a mending kit, and a shower cap.

- Roll items like T-shirts, undergarments, and wrinkle-free clothing to make the best use of space in your suitcase. Items taken from the cleaners can be packed in their plastic covering to avoid wrinkling. Simply remove the hanger and fold the piece of clothing one layer over the other.

Beauty

- Bring only the cosmetics you will definitely use. A good idea is to have one kit that contains all the cosmetics necessary. A New York City company called il-Makiage makes a small two-trayed kit called Express Makeup Model Kit containing twenty-one daytime and evening beauty products. The bottom tray contains nine blushers, highlighters, and eyeliners, and an eyelid base in colors suitable for most color types, and for both day and night use. The top tray contains seven brushes for lips, eyes, and face, waterproof mascara, two pencils for lips and eyes, lipstick in a pot, and a concealer. The kit is the size of a softcover book, and the underside of the top cover is mirrored. It closes with a snap and easily slips in your handbag. The cost is $85 for a basic kit; $125 if you wish to customize the products to your specific coloring. Call (800) 722-1011 to order.

The company also makes a small three-by-two-inch compact containing six lipsticks and lip gloss in a tray (filled with pinks, bronze, and red) so you can mix and match and take with you. The cost is $35.

Another fabulous product called Sheer Tinting Moisturizer serves as a moisturizer with a slight tint so that you can avoid wearing foundation; cost, $20.

- Under-eye cream is a must wherever you go. Apply this under your eyes, as well as around your lips to give them a more plump look.
- Carry a small nail file, nail color remover, and polish. A company called Andra makes nail color remover pads (nonacetone). One pad will clean the polish off ten artificial or natural nails.
- Use sunscreen and a moisturizer daily if you are over middle age, or if you have a sensitive skin. Always use sunscreen in warmer climates.
- Use a mask to refresh your skin after a day's sight-seeing, especially if you are going to change and go out for the evening. If you have dry skin, use a ten- to fifteen-minute moisturizer mask. If you have a combination skin, use a tightening mask on the T-Zone for ten to fifteen minutes.
- In warmer climates bring a small water-filled atomizer to spritz on your hands and face to feel refreshed and avoid dry skin. This is also important to do when you're in an airplane, as the air in the plane is very drying to your skin. It's also important to drink plenty of water or nonalcoholic, noncaffeinated beverages to keep your body well hydrated.

- Avoid wearing makeup on a plane as it will just cause your skin to become drier. Just use moisturizer and a lip balm to avoid chapped lips. Also, use a skin cream on your hands during the flight.
- Always cleanse your skin thoroughly before retiring. Don't sleep with your makeup on. This can cause skin irritation as your skin comes in contact with detergents and bedding materials it is not accustomed to, and this may interact with the makeup on your skin.
- Don't overdo the makeup. Remember, you're on vacation, and that should mean loosening up, even in the makeup department. Do as little fussing as possible. Of course, it may be hard to cut down on cosmetics at this time when you want to look your best. But try it. If you spend too much time thinking about your appearance, it's bound to take away from time better spent paying attention to the day's activities and new friends. A friendly face and a warm, open personality are the best means of meeting people and having a great time.

In conclusion, remember traveling is the best way to learn new things and different ways. It's the vital ingredient in a full, well-rounded life. But you have to help the process by being as astute a traveler as possible. So take your time to read this chapter, digest it, and perhaps reread it before you go. Most of all, use common sense whenever you're in a new place and find yourself faced with awkward or unsettling situations. Don't hesitate to discuss with your tour director or hotel management whatever questions or thoughts you may have. His or her job is to attend to your needs and see that you have the best time possible.

PART II

EVERYTHING YOU NEED TO KNOW ABOUT TOURS

From the perspective of the solo woman traveler, we have found escorted tours to be perfect pathways to a fun, hassle-free vacation. One way for you to raise your comfort level regarding this type of vacation is to think of yourself as being on your way to attend a play in a theater. Quite naturally, you anticipate an enjoyable program. You accept that it is the responsibility of the cast to lift your spirits and bring you pleasure with a pleasing performance. And your part in the overall picture? You pay for your ticket and leave everything to those onstage and behind the scenes.

So it is when you choose a reputable escorted tour. You are purchasing the end result of a lot of hard work. Someone else is concerned with your transportation, getting you to and from the airport, carrying and keeping track of your luggage, making your hotel reservations, planning your itinerary, ensuring that you see all the highlights of the destination, steering you toward the best shops and restaurants, and yet leaving you time to rest and pursue your personal interests.

Most tours include some, if not all, meals. All include the services of professional tour directors who accompany the tour groups and who are usually very personable and well trained in handling the needs of travelers. They are knowledgeable about the destinations and provide you with mini history lessons about places and things you see. Your land transportation is a comfortable, often luxurious motor coach. And forget about standing in line to get tickets. Your visit is arranged months in advance, and your group is ushered to the head of the line at many popular attractions.

Escorted tours offer peace of mind. You have the assurance that your vacation has been planned by professionals who have been there and have assessed the destination. And in the event of a problem, you have the tour director and other members of the tour company to assist you. Also, once you have paid for the tour, you know in advance what other costs there will be and you can plan accordingly.

Tours offer another key benefit, and that is savings. You simply can't beat the prices. By contracting in bulk for hotels, restaurants, ground transportation, and other services, tour operators are able to achieve substantial savings over what an individual can purchase. In addition, tour operators are often able to secure accommodations, airline tickets, and other travel amenities that might be impossible, or very difficult, to obtain on your own.

Of course, purchasing a tour is an important venture that deserves careful consideration. Knowing what to expect can ensure that your holiday is a pleasure, not a disappointment. So choose your tour wisely. Perhaps enlist the aid of a travel agent. We have thoroughly investigated the escorted tour market, and have found myriad destinations, prices, and levels of facilities. When you find a tour company you like, check it out thoroughly.

Don't assume anything. Always ask the following questions:

- Who are the companies offering the tour packages? How long have they been in business? What assurances do they offer?
- What are the demographics of their travelers? If you're traveling solo, you probably don't want to go on a tour that is likely to be all couples.
- Do the prices include airfare? If so, from what city, and is there an add-on fare from your city? If air transportation is not included, do they recommend an airline they work with, and can they get your ticket?
- Will you be met at the airport by the tour operator? Will you be taken to the airport for your return flight?

Regarding the tour itinerary, ask:

- Will it include all the sights you want to see?
- What are the optional excursions, if any, and how much do they cost?

- How much unplanned time is built in to the schedule?
- Is there enough leisure time for your taste or is there too much?
- Are you comfortable with the amount of time spent on the bus and getting from one destination to another?
- How many people will be on the tour? You might prefer going with lots of people or with as few as possible.
- How much walking around will there be? Some people enjoy walking, others don't.

Ask about the accommodations; they're an important consideration. Read the descriptions of the hotels featured. Will they suit your needs? Keep in mind that hotels in foreign countries may not always reflect American standards. Be aware of the location of the hotel. If you are going to have a lot of leisure time you may want a hotel that is centrally located. If you are interested in sharing a room to get the double occupancy rate (the tour price per person, based on two persons sharing a room), ask if the tour operator will match you up with a roommate. Or, if you wish to have single accommodations, ask about the single-room supplement, which is the additional price you pay not to have to share a room.

Meals are, of course, one of the most enjoyable parts of a vacation. Find out how many meals are included each day. What do they consist of? Will they generally reflect the cuisine of the region? If you have special dietary needs, will they be addressed?

Last, but not least, be sure to read the "Conditions" section at the end of the brochure. Make sure you understand the tour company's policy regarding reservations, deposits, cancellation, refunds, and availability of insurance.

Now that you know all about how escorted tours operate, read on and let us help you choose a tour that will fulfill your travel dreams.

5

The Best of Europe and the South Pacific

The man who goes alone can start today.—Thoreau

Europe truly is a must-see, many times! Along with the splendor of their distinctive landscapes, cultures, and languages, most European countries today are a proud combination of remnants of bygone civilizations and thriving, bustling new ventures sprung from the modern world of technology. As such, they make for excellent escorted sight-seeing trips. Ancient ruins, medieval churches, and castles with their towers and domes exist alongside elegant homes, hotels, captivating restaurants, and designer-label shops. This blend of old and new creates an unforgettable experience for visitors. The lands of so many of our forefathers, with all their history, scenic beauty, and diversity of peoples, definitely beckon.

Another exciting vacation destination for single women is the South Pacific (Australia, New Zealand, and Fiji). Australia is a land where expansive horizons take your breath away. It's a land of friendly people, especially the men, who seem to outnumber the women, and are very receptive to the charms of American women. In fact, a number of tour operators told us that on almost every one of their tours to Australia, romance or flirtation blossoms, sometimes even leading to marriage.

Aside from the charms of their male population, a trip to Australia is an experience of enchantment. Known for its kangaroos, koala bears, and other unusual animal and plant life, Australia is a land of contrast and contradictions where tropical rain forests border hot arid deserts, and cosmopolitan cities neighbor places of ancient aboriginal legend.

Numerous tour companies are involved in both the European and South Pacific markets, and based on our research and experience, the tours we mention represent some of the best. Those that give the most value and stand up to their promises, and that we found to be especially comfortable and satisfying experiences for the solo woman traveler, are highlighted with our personal comments.

Collette Tours
180 Midde St.
Pawtucket, RI 02860
(800) 832-4656
www.collettetours.com

With more than eighty years' experience, Collette distinguishes itself as a first-class sight-seeing tour company. Its package tours successfully combine an ideal balance of fully escorted sightseeing, entertainment, and leisure time. While other companies usually offer optional, often expensive extras, Collette tours include everything—even several evenings of entertainment—which tends to make them less costly in the long run. Travelers ride around in clean, comfortable motor coaches driven by knowledgeable, skillful professionals. Tour guides are full-time employees who are intelligent and informative and offer personal assistance.

WHERE—Europe, Australia, New Zealand, and the South Pacific, Hawaii, Alaska, the Continental U.S.A., Canada, South America, Antarctica, Costa Rica, the Orient, China, and Africa.

FELLOW TRAVELERS—Typically, travelers have tended to be fifty-five years old and up, but that is changing, especially on the Costa

Rica tours, which attract many travelers in their thirties and forties. Many single parents traveling with their offspring take the "soft adventure" trips to the U.S. national parks and Costa Rica's rain forest. Single men and women are found on any given tour.

PRICE—$1,049 to $3,199 for single-room accommodations. (This is for European tours; prices vary widely for other destinations.) Airfare is not included.

Imperial Cities, Featuring Vienna, Budapest, Prague (eleven days)

The account of this tour is given from the personal experience of one of the authors. The tour consists of three days in each of these charming, picturesque cities filled with Old-World ambience. Your itinerary includes visits to historic sites, a delightful Danube River cruise, as well as three evenings of entertainment.

The tour begins in Vienna, a city of diverse styles of beautiful architecture, with stops along the ancient streets around St. Stephen's Cathedral and Karntner Strasse, a lively street lined with shops. Another stop is Schoenbrunn, the summer retreat of the Hapsburg dynasty for more than two hundred years. You also visit the luxurious Belvedere Palace, a magnificent compound of elaborate buildings connected by beautiful fountains and gardens.

A relaxing four-hour motor-coach drive takes you to the Hungarian city of Budapest, also famous for the magnificence of its architecture. Budapest is actually two cities, Buda and Pest, connected by the graceful Chain Bridge. Here you see the historic Matthias Church, site of many coronations of kings, and the Fisherman's Bastion with its white walls, towers and arcades, as well as other points of interest. You also explore the Hungarian countryside and the picturesque towns along the Danube bend. There is a visit to the beautiful town of Szentendre, with its baroque churches and charming Main Square. You see the picturesque Hungarian great plain countryside and a typical Puszta horse show demonstrated by the Csikos (Hungarian horsemen). A leisurely ride through the Hungarian agricultural scenic countryside takes you to the Republic of Slovakia for a lunch stop in the capital city of Bratislava.

Your last destination is Prague in the Czech Republic. This is a city of stunning beauty with more than five hundred towers and steeples as well as many parks and gardens. While the capitals of many other Eastern European nations were flattened or heavily damaged during World War II, Prague survived intact. On your Prague walking tour you see such wonders as the Charles Bridge over the Vltava River, lined with its sixteen arches, thirty statues, and lampposts, affording spectacular views of castles and skyline. Other sights are the Teyn Church and its magnificent towers, the unique Astronomical Clock, St. Nicholas Cathedral, and Old Town Hall. You also visit the Old Jewish Quarter with its marvelous synagogues, museums, and cemetery.

This wonderful city is also a mecca for shopping. Everything is available from crystal in all shapes and forms to delightful fairyland marionettes. In addition, Prague has a vibrant nightlife with a jazz and rock scene.

Another highlight is a visit to Kutna Hora, an ancient silver-mining town located in the valley of the Vrchlice River. The Bohemian kings had their residence in the city, and it also was the mint for the "Prague Penny."

MEALS AND ACCOMMODATIONS—The package included nine breakfasts, one lunch, and six dinners that reflect the character of the cities and are of the highest quality. Live music often adds to the festive atmosphere. The four-star hotels capture the feeling of the area while offering comfort and luxury.

FELLOW TRAVELERS—The thirty-one travelers on this tour were a very congenial mix of couples and singles of all ages from all over the United States.

PRICE—$1,399 to $1,459 for double occupancy; $1,999 to $2,054 for single-room accommodations depending on the time of year. Airfare is not included.

PERSONAL COMMENTARY—We highly recommend this tour, which offers travelers an excellent view of cities that depict nearly a thousand years of art and history. The beauty of these cities takes your breath away. Every period of architecture, from Roman to baroque to modern, is extravagantly represented and a feast for the eyes.

The people are friendly, the streets are clean, picturesque, and safe, and the shops are filled with all kinds of interesting items. The food is high quality, fresh with a home-cooked flair, and individual preferences are catered to. One young woman on our tour who would not eat any red meat was able to enjoy delicious vegetarian fare wherever we went.

Your three-night stay in each city allows you to not feel rushed and includes time for relaxation and shopping. The solo woman traveler can take comfort in knowing the guide is always there for her whether she needs to find a local pharmacy or negotiate the best price for some trinket. Our guide was always articulate, witty, helpful, and fluent in a number of languages. Travel from one destination to another was not just nap time. It was informative and interesting, as the guide continually pointed out fascinating sites and explained the history of the area in a witty and thoroughly enjoyable manner. Time on the bus was often a time for socializing, and some evenings we had sing-alongs. During our stretches on the road, our driver always had a store of cold drinks. We soon came to trust our driver's competence, and he was always there with a helpful hand when we were loading and unloading the motor coach.

Our guide said she sees many solo women on this and other Collette tours. Some are a little apprehensive at first, but they soon get into the spirit of things and find friends within the group.

Natural Riches of New Zealand (nineteen days)

After crossing the Pacific Ocean and the international date line (and losing a day), you arrive in the charming city of Christchurch, often called the most English city outside of England. The following day you board the Trans-Alpine Express train for a scenic ride through the Southern Alps. Your journey then continues by motor coach through the picturesque countryside to Mt. Cook National Park where an optional flight-seeing tour is available. You continue on to Dunedin where you enjoy a tour of this lovely city featuring numerous preserved sites of Edwardian architecture.

Other places of interest include Te Anau; a fascinating luncheon cruise on Milford Sound; and the charming town of Queenstown, where you can take an optional jet-boat ride or a special helicopter trip along the Remarkables Mountain Range. You also drive through the Franz Josef Glacier Region to see the snow-capped peaks of the Alps and New Zealand's spectacular coastline. Other stops include Greymouth, Wellington, Rotorua, Bay of Islands, and Auckland where you cruise through the famous Hole In The Rock and view Cape Brett Lighthouse. From Auckland you depart for home, recrossing the international date line and regaining the day you lost at the beginning of your trip.

MEALS AND ACCOMMODATIONS—This trip includes fifteen breakfasts, one lunch, ten dinners, and one dinner with a New Zealand family. You stay at city-centered four- and five-star hotels.

FELLOW TRAVELERS—Both couples and singles take this tour. In the past they usually were men and women fifty-five years and older, but that is changing, and now more young people are attracted to it.

PRICE—$1,699 to $1,799 for double occupancy; $2,399 to $2,499 for single occupancy. Airfare is not included.

Globus & Cosmos
5301 South Federal Circle
Littleton, CO 80123
(800) 851-0728
www.globusandcosmos.com

Globus and Cosmos are owned by the same company. Founded in 1928, Globus has grown into a leading operator of affordable first-class sight-seeing tours. Cosmos is well known for its budget tours. The difference between the two divisions is to be found in their hotel accommodations and what is included in the tours. Cosmos offers less sight-seeing and more optional excursions than Globus. Globus hotels are higher rated than Cosmos.

WHERE—Although Europe is the focus of both tour programs (they say they carry more Americans to Europe than any other operator), both offer tours of the United States., Canada, Mexico, Central and South America, the Orient, and the South Pacific as well.

MEALS AND ACCOMMODATIONS—You will be well-fed on both Globus and Cosmos tours, but because of their excellent prices, don't expect gourmet meals. Globus provides daily buffet and/or continental breakfast in the style of the country and Cosmos a full English breakfast in Britain/Ireland (except London) and continental breakfast on the continent. Dinner is usually not included in major cities. When dinners are included they are three-course hotel meals with a set menu of perhaps two choices. Some regional specialties are served, but generally they try to please the tastes of average tourists who may not be very adventurous. Lunches are rarely included. Guides suggest various places to eat.

All Globus and Cosmos hotels are clean and comfortable. They have considerable variety in their style, character, and decor; you may stay in anything from a centuries-old inn to a modern high-rise. Globus provides superior accommodations. Most hotels have amenities such as satellite TV, minibar, a cocktail lounge, a restaurant, room service, and concierge services. Many also have a swimming pool, health club, shops, and dry cleaning on the premises. Cosmos hotels are chosen for cleanliness, comfort, and best value. They are always in good neighborhoods. The company's brochures list the names and ratings of the hotels reserved for each tour on the individual tour pages. Hotels in Eastern Europe and Russia may not be of the same standard as western hotels with the same official rating.

PRICES—$1,145 to $8,003 for single accommodations. Airfare is included.

FELLOW TRAVELERS—People who take both Globus and Cosmos tours are a broad mix of ages, occupations, and nationalities. About one-third are either single or traveling alone. Globus passengers tend to be a bit older than those on Cosmos, probably because Globus tours are more expensive.

Globus's British Sampler—Impressions of England, Wales, and Scotland (ten days)

The account of this tour is given from one of the author's personal observations. The tour begins in London and includes most of the famous landmarks: Royal Albert Hall, Kensington Palace, Knightsbridge, the Houses of Parliament, Big Ben, the River Thames, and Westminster Abbey. Highlights are visits to St. Paul's Cathedral and Buckingham Palace, where you see the changing of the guard.

Also on the itinerary is a visit to Stonehenge, the prehistoric temple in use about 4,000 years ago and now the most important prehistoric monument in Britain. Another exciting stop is the elegant Georgian city of Bath, where you see the amazing excavations of the Roman Baths. You also visit Stratford-upon-Avon where you see William Shakespeare's home, a well-preserved cottage with its stone flooring still intact, and that of his wife, Anne Hathaway, with its famous, fabulous thatched roof. You continue to Wales with an overnight stop in picturesque Llangollen, and a visit to William Wordsworth's beloved Grasmere.

Then it's on to historic Scotland with a shopping stop at the Moffat Weavers, known for its Scottish knitwear. A highlight of the stop in the city of Edinburgh is at Abbotsford House, the home of the great Scottish writer Sir Walter Scott. Then you drive back to England with a stop at Belvoir Castle; afterward you return to London to get your flight home.

MEALS AND ACCOMMODATIONS—All breakfasts while on tour are included; three are continental, the others full English breakfasts. Also included are four three-course dinners with a choice of menus and coffee. The guide treats everyone to one welcome drink. All the meals are hearty and good. The full breakfasts are especially enjoyable and feature a variety of foods. The continental breakfasts are also very good; they include more of a variety than usual and are served in your room at the time of your preference.

The modern Novotel in London has three restaurants and an interesting gift shop. The rooms tend to be small, but cozy and comfortable. The other hotels—Bath Hilton, Llangollen Hand, Glasgow Jurys, Edinburgh Hilton, and Harrrogate Moat House— are all charming and comfortable. Some of the rooms are very large; some even have canopy beds. All bathrooms are spotless and have blow-dryers.

FELLOW TRAVELERS—As usual on Globus tours, there was a broad range of ages and occupations in this group of thirty people. They included mothers with daughters in their early twenties, a father with his twenty-two-year-old son, and people in their sixties or older. There were also sisters and women friends traveling together, husbands and wives, a single gentleman, and six solo women. Yet everyone enjoyed each other's company. The time spent on the motor coach was never boring.

PRICE—$1,026 to $1,643 for double occupancy; single supplement, $285. Airfare from New York City is included.

PERSONAL COMMENTARY—This tour gives you more than your money's worth. It is well planned and well orchestrated. It's name, British Sampler, is well chosen. You see as much of London, Wales, and Scotland as is possible in the allotted time, and that whets your appetite for a return trip to see more of each location.

This is an ideal tour for the solo woman traveler, especially if it is your first time abroad. Not only are these English-speaking destinations, but the people have similar lifestyles and it's easy to get around on your own. The expertise of our tour guide greatly contributed to our well-being. Our guide was at all times charming, enthusiastic, personable, and professional. Our motor coach was new and comfortable, and the driver was skilled; we felt very safe.

G'Day Australia (fifteen days)

After your transatlantic flight you arrive on day two of the tour in Sydney. You remain in Sydney the following day and visit a wildlife park but have part of the day at leisure. An early evening flight then takes you to Cairns, gateway to the Great Barrier Reef. A spectacular drive along the coastline brings you to the resort town of Port Douglas, when you board a fast catamaran to the Great Barrier Reef for coral viewing from the underwater observatory. Sea snorkeling is available for the adventurous. After one more day at Cairns, you're off on a morning flight to Ayers Rock and then to Alice Springs. Next is the city of Adelaide where early risers have the opportunity to take an optional hot-air balloon ride over the plains at sunset. The following day there is a tour of Adelaide with its beautiful parks and exotic botanic gardens. Next is a short flight to Melbourne where you visit such landmarks as Parliament House and the Shrine of Remembrance. The following two days are spent in Melbourne on your own with a wonderful farewell dinner.

MEALS AND ACCOMMODATIONS—This trip includes thirteen breakfasts, two lunches, and three dinners. You stay at seven hotels that all reflect the charm of the area.

FELLOW TRAVELERS—About one-third are usually single or traveling together, both women and men with a broad mix of ages and occupations.

PRICE—$1,698 to $1,709, land only; $3,226 to $3,670 double occupancy, including air from Los Angeles; single supplement, $698.

Homeric Tours, Inc.
55 East 59th St.
New York, NY 10022
(800) 223-5570 or (212) 753-1100
www.homerictours.com

This company's speciality is tours within Greece, and many are combined with a cruise. They also offer tours to Italy, Turkey, Egypt, Israel, Cyprus, Morocco, Spain, Portugal, and Eastern Europe. Extension packages to Italy, Turkey, Egypt, Israel, and Cyprus can be added to any of their Greek tours.

PRICE—$990 to $3,000 for double occupancy; single supplement, $50 to $570. Airfare is included.

Homeric Wonder (eleven days)

Your trip begins with your arrival in Athens and a day at leisure. The next morning you enjoy a guided tour of Athens with visits to the Acropolis and the world-famous on-site museum. The following day you're on your own, perhaps to shop for bargains at the Athens Flea Market.

The next day your ship takes you to the beautiful whitewashed island of Mykonos. For several decades Mykonos has been a favorite of jet-setters from around the world. After an overnight stay and a morning in Mykonos you board the ship for the continuation of your four-day cruise to the Greek Islands and Turkey. Your port stops during the cruise include Rhodes, Crete, and more, with optional tours available to explore these extraordinary cities.

MEALS AND ACCOMMODATIONS—Four breakfasts in Athens, one lunch, plus all meals aboard the ship. Various categories of hotels are used on this trip, but all are clean and comfortable and reflect the culture of the area. Aboard the ship you have an inside cabin with two lower beds.

FELLOW TRAVELERS—Greece attracts people from all walks of life of all ages, especially singles, due to its swinging nightlife. Mykonos, the heart of the Greek Islands, attracts more singles of all ages than almost any other island in Greece. Its friendly environment is very conducive to socializing.

PRICE—$1,789 to $2,089 for double occupancy; single supplement, $498 to $799. Airfare from New York City is included.

PERSONAL COMMENTARY—Our stay in Greece, arranged by Homeric, was in Mykonos. We found Greece, with its 5,000 years of history and culture, a definite must-see, and this tour company, with its excellent track record, is the one to take you there. Greece is the birthplace of Western civilization and cradle of democracy; it is where art, literature, architecture, science, music, medicine, government, and sportsmanship began many centuries ago.

The Greece of today is a harmonious potpourri of the ancient and the contemporary. It has major archaeological sites, secluded beaches, picturesque ports, and whitewashed villages perched on impressive mountaintops, as well as bustling cities and towns filled with shops, hotels, restaurants, and nightclubs.

We stayed at the San Marco Hotel and highly recommend it. The rooms are luxurious, complete with a blow-dryer, minibar, safe, and direct-dial telephone. We especially enjoyed the serenity of the spectacular sea view from the room. The hotel is beautifully designed in typical Mykonian style, with whitewashed and stone walls, wooden pergolas, and overhanging balconies. With only eighty-six rooms, its size is just right—small enough not to be too commercial and for one to be able to get around easily but large enough to have all amenities, including a tennis court, swimming pool, and gymnasium. The beach of unique rounded stones, which were used by primitive man to make tools, has been declared of great archaeological importance and is, therefore, protected.

Blue Voyages Tours and Travel LLC
323 Geary Street, Suite 401
San Francisco, CA 94102
(800) 81-TURKEY or (800) 818-8753
www.bluevoyage.com

This company offers sight-seeing tours in Turkey and Greece by land and by sea. The owners are Turkish and have much personal knowledge of the country. The company's catalog features eighteen escorted land tours. The company also specializes in sailing/motor boat tours and bare boat chartering (a form of yacht hiring). In addition to their weekly sailing tours they have a boat/land tour featuring the ancient cities of the Turkish Rivera. These tours afford the opportunity to explore the coastal towns and historic sites along the Mediterranean coast of Turkey (also known as the Lycian Coast).

PRICE—$350 to $3,400 for double occupancy; single supplement, $50 to $1,445. Airfare is not included.

Istanbul (eight days)

This tour explores Istanbul's history as well as its colorful daily life. More than 3,000 years old, Istanbul is the protector of the relics of the Byzantine and Ottoman empires in its museums, ancient churches, palaces, mosques, and bazaars. Opera, theater, ballet, and art exhibitions take place all year.

Your tour begins with an exciting full day in the old part of Istanbul, with a visit to the Hippodrome, where chariot races took place in ancient times. Other highlights include visits to the Blue Mosque, a landmark on Sultanahmet Square with its six minarets of beautiful blue tiles, the underground Cistern, the St. Sophia Church, and much more. Another enjoyment is a captivating cruise on the Bosphorus, the impressive waterway dividing Europe and Asia. The itinerary also includes a visit to the architecturally unique Suleymaniye Mosque. For shoppers there is time to explore the two huge Ottoman marketplaces, the Covered Bazaar and the Spice Market, where time stands still. Another stop is the Dolmabahce Palace located on the shores of the Bosphorus. This was the last residence of the Ottoman sultans until the fall of their empire.

On the last two days of your stay in this city, you are on your own to explore as you wish. One good choice is to check out the modern shops in Taksim Square or explore nearby museums. You may also wish to stroll through the narrow streets of the Galata Quarter or visit the famous Pera Palace Hotel that once hosted the travelers of the Orient Express.

MEALS AND ACCOMMODATIONS—Included are six breakfasts, three lunches, and four dinners. You can choose to stay in a deluxe hotel in the new part of Istanbul, near a modern and interesting district open to pedestrians only, or you can stay in a first-class hotel in the middle of the old town of Istanbul.

FELLOW TRAVELERS—Generally there are twenty to twenty-five people on a tour with a mix of couples and singles. Ages range from mid-twenties to mid-sixties and older.

PRICE—This depends on the classification of the hotel of your choice. For a first-class hotel the cost is $775 for double occupancy; single supplement, $205. The deluxe hotel cost is $975 for double occupancy; single supplement, $355. Airfare is not included.

PERSONAL COMMENTARY—Istanbul is a fabulous place to go shopping. Many visitors return just for that reason. Authentic handwoven carpets and kilims made of wool or silk are often great bargains. Traditional Turkish handcrafts are in abundance, including vases, plates, copper and brassware goods, samovars, and hookahs. Istanbul's fabulous Grand Bazaar is a maze of covered streets housing 4,000 shops, cafés, and restaurants. Other shopping areas are: Arasta Bazaar, Spice Bazaar, Atakoy Galleria, and AK Center.

A word of advice: Remember that bargaining is expected in bazaars and in some resort areas. Be careful to know exactly what you are buying.

Trafalgar Tours
11 East 26th St.
New York, NY 10010
(800) 457-6891 or (800) 854-0103
www.trafalgartours.com

Trafalgar is well known in the escorted tour industry as it has been offering excellent value on its sightseeing tours for over fifty years. Tours are planned to give you plenty of free time to relax and pursue your own interests.

WHERE—This company offers 150 trips within the United States and to Britain, Europe, the Middle East, Australia, New Zealand, and the Orient.

PRICE—Trafalgar's Cost Saver Europe & Britain offers a savings of nearly 30 percent over the cost of its first-class tours by featuring "quality superior tourist class" (usually smaller) hotels with private facilities. These tours average $70 per day. Their other programs feature hotels that are first class, superior first class, or selected deluxe. Prices for these tours are more costly; the most expensive costs about $100 per day for a European tour.

Irish Experience (twelve days)

This is a wonderful tour of Ireland taken by one of the authors. The journey begins in Dublin where sight-seeing includes such marvels as St. Patrick's Cathedral, Dublin Castle, and Phoenix Park. Your motor coach then takes you to the Boyne Valley, and via Drogheda you cross the border into Ulster. You also enjoy the views of Carlingford Lough and a scenic drive through the Mountains of Mourne to Downpatrick, arriving in Belfast. Here you see the city hall and much more. Next you travel the Antrim Coast road, seeing charming castles along the way. An interesting stop is at Bushmills, the oldest whiskey distillery in the world. From here you visit the huge basalt columns rising from the sea known as the Giant's Causeway. Back on your motor coach you go to Londonderry for more sight-seeing, including the city walls, which are some of the best preserved in Europe. Then you visit the famous Belleek Pottery factory.

Afterward you arrive at Sligo. Your travels in this area take you through Yeats country to the lakes and mountains of Connemarra and then on to Galway Bay. From there you travel south via Ennis to Limerick with a tour of the city that shows you St. Mary's Cathedral, King John's Castle, and the Treaty Stone. There is also time for excursions on your own. Next you go to Killarney where you enjoy the spectacular scenery on your drive round the Ring of Kerry with its plunging cliffs, lush lakeland, granite mountains, and sandy beaches.

Next you go to county Cork, stopping at Blarney Castle for a chance to kiss the stone and acquire the "gift of gab." Then you pass through the town of Cork on your way to Youghal and along the scenic coast to Waterford, home of the famous crystal, with a chance to visit the Waterford factory and buy to your heart's content. From here it's on to Kilkenny and then back to Dublin for your return trip home.

MEALS AND ACCOMMODATIONS—Ten full hearty Irish breakfasts are included and six table d'hôte three-course dinners. You also are invited to have a welcome drink with your tour director. You stay in first-class hotels.

FELLOW TRAVELERS—This trip included couples and singles, both men and women from all walks of life.

PRICE—$1,640 to $1,725 for double occupancy; single supplement, $230. Trafalgar will match same-sex travelers to avoid the single supplement. Airfare from New York City is included.

PERSONAL COMMENTARY—You have to see Ireland to believe how pretty it is, and Trafalgar's well-planned itinerary showed it to perfection. Ireland's unique charm is felt everywhere on this journey. Its incredible gorgeous greenery is never to be forgotten. The castles and scenic coastal drives are breathtaking, and you enjoy spectacular views all through your trip.

This is an excellent trip for the solo woman traveler because Ireland is an English-speaking country and the Irish are very friendly. You can't help but enjoy their gift of gab wherever you go. Our group was very congenial, and many people paired off to have lunch together during the day.

For those who love shopping, Ireland has much to offer. I don't think there was anyone on the trip who didn't enjoy the stops to buy tweeds, pottery, crystal, and much more. We also had plenty of free time to relax and explore on our own.

The seven hotels on the itinerary are all clean, comfortable, and well chosen. Our guide was at all times well informed and provided interesting information during the entire tour. The motor coach was luxurious, with reclining seats and panoramic windows and an on-board washroom. This is an Irish experience, to be sure.

We conclude this chapter with the hope that we have raised your comfort level regarding escorted tours. They definitely are ideal mixers, and you're bound to find interesting travel companions. Their all-inclusive nature makes them perfect for the solo woman traveler.

Now that you are an expert regarding escorted tours, and have become acquainted with some of our favorites, all you have to do is choose the tour to the destinations of your dreams.

Do remember to keep this book readily available whenever you are planning a journey. Refer to it often. With all this information at hand you can't help but have the time of your life on your holiday!

6

Finding Romance on Singles Tours

*If you never did, you should. These things are fun,
and fun is good.*—Dr. Seuss

If you're young, full of fun, and want to let your hair down, there's a travel opportunity waiting for you! Today vacations galore beckon to younger singles to take to the open road. From tours featuring thrilling adventures in glorious mountainous terrain to trendy tropical escapes, to high-energy and more leisurely paced sight-seeing, there are unique getaways just for the youthful voyager. And forget about breaking your bank account—vacation managers are savvy enough to keep prices affordable for the budget-conscious younger traveler. Today's younger travelers can forget about backpacking, staying at youth hostels, or traveling with a Eurailpass.

If it's romance you're looking for, well, how can you avoid it when you're around young people like yourself? Many of these vacations are just sheer adrenaline from start to finish. They're not for kids and they're not for oldies, they're just for you.

Contiki Tours
2300 E. Katella Ave.
Suite 450
Anaheim, CA 92806
(800) CONTIKI (266-8454)
www.contiki.com

If you're between the ages of eighteen and thirty-five with visions of a fun-filled vacation in some distant land dancing in your head, but your pocketbook brings you back to reality, Contiki Holidays' tour packages can save the day. And if your fantasies also run to romance on the road, Contiki may also fit the bill. Carrying more than 70,000 young men and women annually, the company is the world's largest tour operator of affordable vacations just for this age group. Best of all, about 70 percent of Contiki travelers are single. Contiki itineraries include the highlights of a city and the hot spots but still leave you time enough to explore on your own.

WHERE—Thirty-five different countries, including Europe, North America, Africa, Australia, and New Zealand.

MEALS AND ACCOMMODATIONS—You can choose either a "budget" or a "superior" vacation. Budget accommodations are often dormitory-style, with four people sharing a room and facilities. Accommodations may be quite luxurious—for example, a beautiful chateau in France with a swimming pool—but the drawback (if you see it that way) is sharing the facilities. All breakfasts and half of the dinners are included. Accommodations for the superior European tours are tourist three-star hotels with private facilities, with all breakfasts and dinners included. According to the tour operator, most Americans prefer superior packages because of the private facilities.

PRICE—$349, not including airfare, to $4,580, including airfare from New York City. Prices are based on twin accommodations. Single supplements are not always available. They will provide a roommate as required.

Spain, Portugal, and Gibraltar (fourteen days)

This tour begins with your arrival in Madrid and a day free to explore the Spanish capital. You continue to Cordoba with sightseeing stops, including the Mosque of the Caliphs. Then it's on to the grand hilltop town of Granada, which is noted for the Alhambra, residence of the Moorish kings. The other destinations include Torremolinos on the Costa del Sol, the most lively and popular Mediterranean resort, Seville, and the Rock of Gibraltar. In Lisbon, the capital city of Portugal, you get plenty of time to explore. You also visit the Serra d'Aire Mountains and the famous Fatima shrine. Next stop is the university city of Salamanca, and then on to the walled city of Avila. Finally, it's back to Madrid. The next day it's time to say *adios* as the tour ends after breakfast.

MEALS AND ACCOMMODATIONS—You stay at superior first-class hotels based on your choice of double- or triple-occupancy rooms. These are centrally located hotels with private baths and restaurant facilities on the premises. They are clean, comfortable, and usually charming, with English-speaking staff. A continental breakfast is included each day and half of the dinners. On the days when dinner is not included, an optional night out with dinner is offered.

FELLOW TRAVELERS—Your companions will likely be young professionals—about 60 percent women.

PRICE—$1,225 to $1,739, depending on the time of year; single supplement, $279. Airfare is included. For a triple share there is a reduction of 5 percent off the land price.

Australia—Beaches and Reefs (fourteen days)

The tour begins in Sydney with a night stop right on the beach at Coffs Harbour. Here you can swim, work out in the gym, or play ball while getting to know your fellow travelers. Continuing north, you stop at Australia's most easterly point, Cape Byron, where you may see migrating whales. Then it's on to the premier holiday destinations of Queensland and Surfers Paradise Resort, where you enjoy two days. From there you make a brief stop in Queensland's capital, Brisbane, before heading north to Noosa on Queensland's Sunshine Coast. A launch takes you to Fraser Island, and if it's August, September, or October you can cruise out to Hervey Bay where you might see whales. You then cross the Tropic of Capricorn to your accommodations near the coastal village of Yeppoon. From there you travel to your resort on Long Island in the beautiful Whitsundays for two days of relaxation. Afterward it's time to head back to the mainland and on to Townsville. Here you can visit the Great Barrier Reef Wonderland and its Omnimax theater, and visit an Aussie pub to meet the locals. Crossing over to Magnetic Island, you explore the island suburb of Townsville. From there it's on to Cairns with an opportunity to go white-water rafting on the Tully River en route.

Other highlights include Port Douglas, with time for an optional cruise to see the magnificent coral formations of the Outer Barrier Reef and the dancers of the Tjapukai Aboriginal Cultural Park. You also have the option to try Cairns' newest attraction—the Skyrail, which takes you high above the rain forest canopy to Kuranda. You return to the resort, where the tour ends.

MEALS AND ACCOMMODATIONS—Included are five breakfasts and three dinners; eleven nights in special four-person share in Contiki accommodations (twin-share is also available); two nights at the Surfers Paradise Resort.

FELLOW TRAVELERS—Eighteen- to thirty-five-year-old couples and singles from all over the world.

PRICE—$2,380 to $2,534 for quad-share; $255, twin-share supplement. Airfare from Los Angeles is included.

European Impressions (nineteen-day tour of ten countries)

This tour is a great way to discover Europe. It begins with your arrival in London. You continue your journey to the White Cliffs of

Dover, cross the English Channel to France, and stop in Paris long enough to shop on the Champs Elysées and stroll by the Seine. From Paris you travel to the wine-producing town of Bordeaux. Next you journey to Spain and the fascinating city of Barcelona. You then travel back to France and take a spectacular drive along the French Riviera, with a stop in Monaco, where you see the Royal Palace and visit a casino. Italy is next, with stops in Pisa (the Leaning Tower) and Baptistry. Next it's on to Tuscany, with its olive groves and vineyards, and then Florence and Venice. Your complimentary motorboat tour takes you to St. Mark's Square and other Venetian landmarks. Your journey continues to Austria's picturesque town of Innsbruck, and then to the Bavarian capital of Munich in Germany. Your next country is Switzerland via the tiny principality of Liechtenstein. You spend two nights in Lauterbrunnen, set in the heart of the Swiss Alps. You visit Lucerne with time to shop before leaving Switzerland and reentering Germany, arriving in the student city of Heidelberg on the banks of the Neckar River. Leaving Germany, you travel through the tiny country of Luxembourg to Belgium and its capital, Brussels. Then you return to France for your cross-channel ferry back to London.

MEALS AND ACCOMMODATIONS—The package includes sixteen continental breakfasts and eight dinners. Accommodations are in superior tourist-class hotels, based on your choice of twin- or triple-share with private facilities.

PRICES—$1,670 to $2,100 depending on the time of year; single supplement, $360; triple-share reduction, 5 percent off the land tour. Airfare is included.

GORPtravel
10055 Westmoor Dr., Suite 215
W. Minster, CO 80021
(877) 440-GORP
www.gorptravel.com

This company offers North American backcountry and Old West dude ranch adventures. The majority of the trips last one week or less. This company recently expanded its offerings to include a number of trips exclusively for singles/solos. Vacations include creative multiactivity adventures (hiking, rafting, biking, climbing); saddle adventures (horseback trips, wagon trains, cowboy cattle drives, and roundups); adventures afoot (wilderness walking, hiking, trekking, and climbing); scuba diving and snorkeling, and more.

If you wish to go on a tour for singles and solos only, state this when you call to make your reservation.

WHERE—United States, British Columbia, Mexico, Honduras, Belize.

PRICE RANGE—$800 to $2,500; single supplement, 15 to 25 percent additional. Airfare is not included.

Colorado Mountain Sports Week (five days)

This is an educational adventure in Colorado offering an array of outdoor activities, including horseback riding, rafting, biking, and climbing. You meet in Colorado Springs and head out to the rustic Bear Basin Ranch where you pick up your tent. You're then off for a day of basic climbing instruction under the watchful eye of a seasoned guide. The next morning you head to the corral for lessons on horsemanship, followed by two days of riding the open range and woodlands. Then, it's up to the hills on mountain bikes, pedaling deep into the rugged Sangre de Cristo range. Your last day is spent on the Arkansas River enjoying a paddle raft trip through Browns Canyon.

MEALS AND ACCOMMODATIONS—Three hearty meals a day are included.

FELLOW TRAVELERS—Singles and couples twenty-five to forty-five years old.

FITNESS LEVEL—All adventures are fairly moderate with some offering advanced options. Every trip has plenty of flexibility for less challenging routes and activities to accommodate a wide range of abilities.

PRICE—$925. Airfare is not included.

New Mexico Sampler (six days)

This adventure begins in Sante Fe, New Mexico, and explores the peaceful forest trails, remote back roads, centuries-old villages, and meandering river canyons of northern New Mexico. The region between Santa Fe and Taos is noted for its natural beauty, intriguing blend of Native American, Spanish, and Anglo cultures, ancient pueblos, fine restaurants, and distinctive lodgings. The trip's highlights include a hike into the Pecos Wilderness, biking along Rio Chiquito and Cabresto Creek, rafting on the Rio Grande, and a sensational walk to the base of Mt. Wheeler, the state's highest peak.

MEALS AND ACCOMMODATIONS—All meals are included except one lunch and one dinner. Your meals have a southwestern flair. Inns are chosen for their character and historical aspects, reflecting the culture and style of the area.

FELLOW TRAVELERS—Singles and solo travelers between the ages of twenty-five and forty-five.

FITNESS LEVEL—Moderate, with some advanced options.

PRICE—$1,650; mountain bike rental, $125. There is an additional charge for horseback riding. Airfare is not included.

Glacier Multisport—Bike, Hike, and Raft (six days)

If you're looking for an alpine experience to surpass all others, try this one to Glacier National Park, where jagged peaks soaring skyward and vibrant wildflowers mingle with grizzly bears munching berries in the afternoon sun. The park's wealth of natural attractions is endless, and you can use every means possible to reach the next forest, vista, or historic alpine lodge. You can trek to the tops of lofty ridges and raft the lively Flathead River. You can hug rugged mountainsides with two fat tires. In the heart of this living masterpiece wilderness, life takes on a new meaning.

WHERE—Montana, Glacier National Park. The trip departs from West Glacier.

MEALS AND ACCOMMODATIONS—All meals except one are included. Inns are chosen for their character and charm.

FELLOW TRAVELERS—Singles and solo travelers between the ages of twenty-five and forty-five.

FITNESS LEVEL—Moderate with some advanced options.

PRICE—$1,998 for twin accommodations; single supplement, $560; bike rental, $60. Airfare is not included.

Super Clubs
Hedonism II
2021 Hayes St.
Hollywood, FL 33020
(800) GO-SUPER (417-8737)
www.superclub.com

Super Clubs offer a number of different all-inclusive tropical vacations. Their Hedonism II vacation is a resort vacation set on twenty-three acres of a tropical paradise for people who want a nonstop all-out party. If you want to eat and drink, love and laugh, party and play around the clock, this is the place to do it. Everything you can eat, drink, and do is included. And tipping is not permitted so you never have to think about money. All you do have to think about at this resort is what to do next. And when and with whom. Activities include water sports (swimming, snorkeling, water-skiing, sailing, kayaks, windsurfing, and more); land sports (tennis, basketball, bicycling, jogging, golf, cricket, and more); and a vast array of special events including pajama parties, mixology and reggae classes, glass-bottom boat rides, tropical shows, karaoke, and more. There's also a fully equipped fitness center, including aerobic classes. Secluded hammocks for two are hidden about the grounds. There are two beaches, one nude and one not. The resort has a boutique, pharmacy, and duty-free shop.

MEALS AND ACCOMMODATIONS—All meals are included. Buffet-style breakfast, lunch, and dinner are served in the main dining terrace. Super snacks are served from early morning to late at night. Hors d'oeuvres are served from 6 to 7:00 P.M. Rooms have twin beds or king-size beds.

FELLOW TRAVELERS—Young singles (over eighteen) and couples who enjoy partying.

PRICES—For a minimum three-night stay the price ranges from $582 per person for rooms that open to the garden-side (this may be higher during the peak season) to $672 for rooms facing the nude beach; single supplement, $100.

Trafalgar Tours
11 East 26th St.
New York, NY 10010
800 (457-6891)
www.trafalgartours.com

In addition to its other tour packages, Trafalgar offers its Club Breakaway Vacations, a program of vacations for people aged twenty-one to thirty-eight. These tours are designed by people in this age group to guarantee that they are definitely your kind of vacation experience.

WHERE—Europe and the Middle East (England, Netherlands, Germany, France, Switzerland, Italy, Spain, Greece)

PRICE—$950 to $1,999; single supplement, $410. Airfare is not included. Air and land packages are also available. There is a 5 percent reduction for triple-shared rooms.

Taste of Europe (sixteen days)

The exciting destinations on this tour include England, France, Switzerland, Italy, Austria, Germany, and Holland.

Your trip begins in London with a sight-seeing tour. In France your tour includes views of the Eiffel Tower, the Champs Elysées, and a visit to Nôtre Dame Cathedral. Driving through the Burgundy vineyards of central France you enter Switzerland and see the beautiful lakeside city of Lucerne. Then it's on to Milan and Rome where your sight-seeing includes the Forum, Colosseum, and St. Peter's Basilica in the Vatican. You also visit Florence and Venice. The journey continues to Austria's Innsbruck and then there's beer and fun in Germany's famous city of Munich. In Holland you visit a diamond-polishing factory and then return to London and home.

MEALS AND ACCOMMODATIONS—A welcome drink with the tour director is offered in Paris. Continental breakfast is served daily, and six dinners are included. Hotels are superior tourist class with private baths.

PRICE—$1,299 for double occupancy; single supplement, $410. Airfare is not included. Price for air and land is $1,804 to $1,949 depending on when you go.

7

Women-Only Tours

*Only those who risk going too far can possibly find
out how far one can go.*—T. S. Eliot

Whether your taste runs to self-coddling vacations or rejuvenating adventures, there's a gals-only trip for you. And many women are choosing to travel in exclusively female groups. Whether they're footloose and free, divorced, widowed, or, for one reason or another, taking off without their mate or significant other, women are welcoming the opportunity to enjoy themselves in the company of their own sex. Traveling with other women is great fun, like having a big-girl sleepover party. Getting away with just women eliminates the sense of competition; you can let your hair down. No one's out to prove anything. A special camaraderie takes place among women travelers, as well as a feeling of safety traveling as a female group.

Women who travel together often report the rapport they develop turns them into lifelong travel companions. When you go the "ladies only" way, you will be on your own, but never alone.

Wild Women Adventures
152 Bloomfield Rd.
Sebastopol, CA 95472
(800) 992-1322
www.wildwomenadv.com

This tour operator offers an eclectic array of stylish getaways. The company, whimsically subtitled Insanity With Dignity World Tours, was started by two women who based it on the premise that women need to get out more. Trips include special themes such as golf, scuba diving, art, writing, music, cooking, and shopping. The company says it takes women to places off the beaten track to really get to know the local folk. The sight-seeing pace is relaxed, and the planned activities are cultural and social.

WHERE—Thailand, Egypt, Europe, Africa, Mexico.

PRICE—$1,465 to $5,650; single supplement, $207 to $913. Airfare is included.

The Thiam of Your Life (sixteen days)

This is an exotic tour to Thailand. From the hustling and bustling city of Bangkok, tour participants travel north through ethereal scenery to Chiang Mai, home of the elephant camps, exotic Hill tribes, and the largest concentration of cottage handcraft industries in the world (translation: SHOPPING). The tour finishes in the south of the island of Phuket, which is fringed with white sand beaches and surrounded by lush green hills. You can lie on the beach, kayak through limestone caves, or take a class in Thai cuisine.

MEALS AND ACCOMMODATIONS—Daily breakfast is included, as well as six dinners and six lunches. Your hotel is the Marriott Royal Garden Riverside Hotel, a five-star low-rise hotel with the ambience of a resort on the banks of the Chao Phraya River (the River of Kings). The tour also includes an overnight on a cruise vessel in an air-conditioned cabin, the Westin Chiang Mai Hotel in Chiang

Mai, and the Boathouse, a charming boutique hotel on picture-perfect Kata Beach.

FELLOW TRAVELERS—Women from many lifestyles, professional women, homemakers, married, widowed, divorced, and single. Age ranges from women in their twenties to seventies. Forty- and fifty-somethings are in the majority. The maximum number on tours is twelve to sixteen.

PRICE—$3,950 to $4,250 (depending on the city of departure) for double occupancy; single supplement, $575. Airfare from your hometown is included.

Adventure Women
15033 Kelly Canyon Rd.
Bozeman, MT 59715
(800) 804-8686
www. adventurewomen.com

This company offers adventure trips that are broken into winter, spring, summer, and fall athletic categories. Winter adventures feature everything from downhill skiing, whale watching, rafting, and sailing to an African safari. Spring adventures include various types of on-foot tours—trekking, hiking, walking. Summer adventures feature hiking, horseback riding through a desert, and rafting. Fall adventures include walking in rain forests and along coastlines, hiking, sea kayaking, and trekking. Trips are for women over thirty. The average age is fifty.

WHERE—The American West, Europe, Asia, South and Central America, Iceland.

FITNESS LEVEL—There's something for everyone, with trips rated "easy," "moderate," or "high energy."

PRICE—$1,500 to $6,900 for double occupancy; no single supplement is available (they will provide a roommate). Some trips include airfare; others don't.

Sea Kayaking In the Sea of Cortez (Gulf of California) and Espiritu Santo Island, Baja, Mexico (six days)

Your adventure takes place in the Sea of Cortez in the Gulf of California and the enchanted, uninhabited island of Espiritu Santo in Mexico. Tour participants meet at LAX airport for a flight to La Pa, Baja Mexico, and an overnight hotel stay. The following day you board a forty-foot boat for a three-hour journey to the island of Espiritu Santo. For three days you kayak, snorkel, fish, hike, bird-watch, and relax along the shores of this enchanted island. Guided kayak excursions of two to three hours are offered each day to outlying islands, through sea arches, along volcanic cliffs and deserted beaches.

This sea kayak trip is designed to teach you the skills necessary to become a confident paddler. Unlike the classic racing-style kayaks, sea kayaks are made of fiberglass and are quite large and very stable. They take less effort to handle and are easier to steer than canoes.

The Sea of Cortez is home to eight hundred species of fish, several species of dolphins, and sea lions. It is a sanctuary for ring-tailed cats, black jack rabbits, reptiles, over forty species of birds, and a bizarre and fascinating community of desert flora. The tour ends with an overnight hotel stay back in La Paz and a stroll in this colorful town.

MEALS AND ACCOMMODATIONS—All meals are included, plus two nights of double-occupancy hotel accommodations in La Paz. Your other accommodations are a "safari camp." A large dome serves as kitchen and dining hall in inclement weather. Two-person tents provide double-occupancy accommodations, or you may choose to sleep on the beach under the starry sky; a sleep kit is provided, which includes a sleeping bag, a clean liner sheet, and a pad. A portable toilet is used in camp, and bathing is available daily in the sea using a biodegradable soap that lathers in salt water. Fresh water in a sun shower is available for a quick rinse to complete the process.

FELLOW TRAVELERS—Women over thirty; the average age is late forties to early fifties.

FITNESS LEVEL—This trip is rated easy/moderate. However, due to the demands of this journey, you must be in good health and in good physical condition.

PRICE—$1,695 for double occupany; no single supplement is available. Airfare from Los Angeles is included.

Women in the Wilderness
566 Ottawa Ave.
St. Paul, MN 55107-2550
(651) 227-2284

Both high-adventure and "easy power lounging" vacations are offered by this tour operator. Canoeing is their speciality and passion, and they've been doing it for more than thirty years. Another speciality is dogsledding trips. You drive your own team. You learn to communicate with the dogs and enjoy exhilarating runs on wilderness trails. Women in the Wilderness also does sailing, nature study trips, and a number of special-interest trips each year, including writers' workshops, retreats for cancer survivors, elders trips, and some high-adventure canoe trips. This operator's philosophy is to have fun along with learning and adventure.

The Cancer Survivors' Retreat (cosponsored by North Memorial Hospital's Cancer Center) includes snowshoeing, cross-country skiing, dogsled rides, and always good talk. There are no "therapy groups," but there is a lot of support from women sharing their experiences and from the peace of the natural world, they say.

WHERE—Many of the tours are in Minnesota, the company's home state. The tours take you off the typical tourist path and provide you with insight into the history and culture of northern Minnesota. Because there is almost always good snow through mid-March, many of the winter trips are in the Arrowhead region of Minnesota, a four- to five-hour drive from Minneapolis–St. Paul (an hour from

Duluth, the nearest airport). There are also trips to the states of Utah, Wisconsin, and Alaska, and to Canada, Mexico, and Peru.

FELLOW TRAVELERS—Beginners and seasoned travelers; women in their twenties to sixties and up. While some women sign on with a family member or friend, most sign up alone, knowing they will meet compatible fellow travelers.

FITNESS LEVEL—The tour operator says you don't have to be very physically fit. Unless they say a specific trip requires previous experience, or a high level of fitness, it doesn't. There is a trip for everyone. Someone at the company will gladly talk to you and let you know what trip suits your particular abilities and energies.

PRICE—$200 to $3,600 for double occupancy; single supplement is not usually available. Airfare is not usually included, but some prices do include air.

Alaska Canoe Trip on the Noatak River (fifteen days)

This is a natural history expedition above the Arctic Circle, cosponsored by Equinox Expeditions of Alaska. Your journey is an unforgettable canoeing and hiking trip through the Arctic tundra and mountains. The trip covers the first two hundred miles of the Noatak River, which meanders over four hundred miles through undisturbed wilderness. In the headwaters the river is fast, narrow, and shallow. There are a couples of stretches of Class II rapids (nothing very tricky; novices have done this trip). As the river grows, the current gets faster. It is not technically a white-water river, but there are stretches of standing waves. There is also time for hiking around in the upper valley.

MEALS AND ACCOMMODATIONS—Meals are healthy and hearty. However, due to weight and space limits, don't expect gourmet food. The company sends you a food survey to try to accommodate your preferences. Cooking is done on white-gas stoves. If you have your own tent, that's fine, but it's not required. All equipment is supplied.

FELLOW TRAVELERS—Experienced northern travelers and hardcore canoeists, as well as novices, of all ages.

FITNESS LEVEL—You don't have to be a canoeist, but you should be fit and healthy, the kind of person who welcomes new challenges. And you should be prepared to weather the stresses of wind, cold, insects, and lack of privacy.

PRICE—$2,950 for double occupancy; no single supplement is available—therefore you must have a roommate or pay double. The price includes all internal flights from Fairbanks to the expedition site. Airfare to Alaska is not included.

The Lively Art of Mushing

This unusual experience takes place in Wintermoon, Superior National Forest, which is fifty miles northeast of Duluth, Minnesota. You'll learn to harness and run a dog team. Liking dogs is crucial, as is having a generally sturdy body and spirit. The dogs are frisky and enjoy playing with you. When you're not running dogs, you can go snowshoeing or skiing, or simply spend time warming up by the woodstove and watching for the colorful winter birds. In the evening there is plenty of talking, walking under the stars, and relaxing in the sauna. Musher Kathleen Anderson will share her deep interest in the wild animals of the neighborhood.

MEALS AND ACCOMMODATIONS—The lifestyle is simple, as are the meals. Sleeping accommodations consist of a wood-heated bunkhouse. You need to bring a sleeping bag and, if you wish, a pillow. A bit of luxury is available—you can arrange for a therapeutic massage in Two Harbors. A Finnish sauna is used for washing and relaxing.

FELLOW TRAVELERS—Maximum group size is eight, all ages.

FITNESS LEVEL—Dogsledding is challenging, but the trips are not endurance tests. You won't get pushed beyond what you feel comfortable with, but you are encouraged to come in the best shape you can. The more flexible and conditioned you are, the easier it will be and the more fun you'll have.

PRICE—$350 to $495. Airfare is not included.

Adventures For Women
15 Victoria Lane
Morristown, NJ 07960
(973) 644-3592
adventuresforwomen.org

This company offers adventures in walking and hiking. Their get-away options are for as short as a day or weekend and as long as ten days. The company also offers contemplation weekends (designed for women of all ages to share the wisdom of the generations). The philosophy of this program is to promote personal growth through wilderness challenges. The goal is to give women a foundation in outdoor and interpersonal skills and to foster participation in decision making with confidence.

WHERE—The Adirondack Mountains and Catskills Mountains in New York, various locations in New Jersey (classes), and this year in Austria. The company offers different trips to various locations each year.

PRICE—$100 to $200 for a day trip; $300 to $500 for a weekend; $2,500 to Austria, including air; no single supplement is available.

Austria—Hiking the Vorarlberg Alps (fourteen days)

If you love hiking, this strenuous and exhilarating vacation is tailior-made for you. It includes six days of vigorous hiking in the Rheintal region near Lake Constance at an elevation of 3,000 ft., and the Vorarlberg Alps near Schruns, elevation up to 8,000 ft. But your feet do get somewhat of a respite. You also enjoy two full days of sight-seeing in Vienna along with a classical concert at the Schonbrunn Castle. Two rest days are spent traveling by train to Schruns and Vienna. The remaining days are spent traveling from place to place on a comfortable bus.

MEALS AND ACCOMMODATIONS—Daily buffet breakfasts and dinners are included, along with six trail lunches during your hikes. Your lodgings are at charming small hotels within walking distance of public transportation.

FELLOW TRAVELERS—The age range is thirties to sixties. There is a mix of single and married women.

FITNESS LEVEL—You should be physically fit for this trip. The tour operator advises you to prepare for this trip by doing regular walking and hiking, including hills, in the two months before the trip.

PRICE—$2,400 for double occupancy. Airfare is not included, but Adventures for Women will arrange your airfare, which costs about $1,200. The entire group departs from Newark, New Jersey.

The Woman's Travel Club
21401 NE 38th Ave.
Aventura, FL 33180
(800) 480-4448
womenstravelclub.com

This organization offers a variety of trips to their members ($35 membership fee). Trips range from two days to three weeks. Boasting over 1,000 members, they say they are the largest of their kind in the United States. Members come from four foreign countries and many states. Their itineraries focus on the interests of women travelers, and each trip is developed with the help of members who are looking for something more personal when they travel, including visits to private homes. A monthly newsletter informs members about upcoming trips.

WHERE—United States, Europe, Canada, Africa

PRICE—$350 to $4,500 for double occupancy; single supplement, $150 to $750; Airfare is included with most trips.

Pleasures of Provence, France (ten days)

You are met at Marseilles Airport and transferred to the town of Nimes and your hotel. The next day you travel to Arles, the one-time home of Vincent Van Gogh, where you take a walking tour with stops that evoke many important incidents of his life. Another excursion is through one of the wildlife preserves of the Camargue, with a stop at a traditional manade to view the wild horses and bulls rounded up by "gardians"—Camargue cowboys who wear handsome wide-brimmed black hats. You continue to Avignon for a four-night stay, with a museum stop along the way and time to view the medieval city of Les Baux de Provence. Along with much more sight-seeing, there is time for shopping in fine boutiques. Everything you could want in Avignon is within walking distance. Then it's on to Aix-en-Provence, one of the prettiest towns in France, with streets lined with elegant seventeenth-century mansions and more fountains than anyone can count. You have an entire day to explore Aix. You depart for home from the Marseilles Airport.

MEALS AND ACCOMMODATIONS—Daily breakfast, six dinners, and one lunch are included. The meals are typically French and include wine and mineral water. Hotels are all three- and four-star.

FELLOW TRAVELERS—There are usually between twenty and twenty-five women in a group. Includes women of all ages from all walks of life.

PRICE—$2,300 for double occupancy; single supplement, $450. Airfare from Cinncinnati returning to New York is included. The company will arrange for connecting flights at your expense.

Women Traveling Together
1642 Fairhill Dr.
Edgewater, MD 21037
(800) 795-7135
www.women-traveling.com

This is a travel club for women. Membership costs $35 a year. A wide variety of trips are offered, from high-adventure treks to totally pampered vacations. Their options change each year. The club will provide you with a roommate if you want to avoid paying the single supplement.

WHERE—The United States, Europe, Western Canada and Vancouver, and the Mediterranean Islands.

An Intimate Look at Spain and Portugal (fifteen days)

On this wonderful trip you spend five nights in Madrid, three nights in Seville, and five nights in Portugal. Your tour begins in Madrid, the capital of Spain, with a day of sight-seeing. You also visit the cities of Toledo and Cuenca, famous for its "hanging houses," which seem to perch in midair at the edge of the cliff. Other points of interest include the towns of El Escorial, Avila, and Segovia. A train ride then takes you to Barcelona where you enjoy a city tour. You return to Madrid with a day on your own, perhaps to explore the Prado Museum. Next, you take a train to Seville where you have time to explore this beautiful city. You continue by motor coach to Portugal where you arrive in the town of Elvas. You spend several days exploring the highlights of Portugal, and then you fly home from the capital city of Lisbon.

MEALS AND ACCOMMODATIONS—All breakfasts and ten dinners are included. Your accommodations are in "pousadas," historic lodgings that reflect the history and heritage of Spain and Portugal. All rooms have private baths.

FELLOW TRAVELERS—There is a maximum of sixteen people in the group. They are women of all ages from all walks of life.

PRICE—$3,250 for double occupancy; single supplement, $575. Airfare is not included.

Sierra Club Outings
85 Second St., 2nd Floor
San Francisco, CA 94105
(415) 977-5522
www.sierraclub.org/outings

This nonprofit organization offers 330 trips to members (membership rates vary from $19 to $1,000 depending on membership category, age, and income). From Alaska to the Adirondacks, club members work together in their communities to prevent the destruction of natural habitats and to preserve priceless wildlands. Their adventure vacation programs include bicycle riding, camping, hiking, canoeing and kayaking, birding, backpacking, fishing, and rafting. They also have women-only adventure programs.

WHERE—The United States, Latin America, China, Canada, Africa, Europe.

PRICE—$250 to $4,000 for double occupancy; single supplement varies according to the number of people in the group and location. Airfare is not included.

Women's Beginner Backpack: Ansel Adams Wilderness, Sierra Nevada, Calif. (seven days)

This is a hiking trip in the Ansel Adams Wilderness in Sierra Nevada, California. The hike covers territory along creeks that flow over granite slopes and through forests to lakes, with plenty of time to enjoy this little-used area just south of Yosemite Park. Some days the group reaches the campsite by noon and spends the afternoon hiking without a pack, botanizing, sketching, or just enjoying the view. This is a relatively easy trip. Elevations range from 7,000 to 10,000 feet. The total distance is about thirty miles, with one layover day. This is not many miles, but some of them will be scrambling over boulders, talus, and scree slopes, so that the travel itself will be as exciting as each day's destination. The trip includes reading topographical maps, planning trail and cross-country routes, picking campsites, cooking on small stoves, starting campfires, using tarps, and minimizing the group's impact on the fragile terrain.

MEALS AND ACCOMMODATIONS—All meals are included. High-carbohydrate cereals, pasta, crackers, and dried fruit make up the bulk of the meals, with cheese, nuts, and chicken adding a small amount of protein and fat. The easy recipes for soup and one-pot dinners allow even beginners to become four-star wilderness chefs. You need to bring a sleeping bag to keep you warm in freezing weather (temperatures range from eighties during the day to thirties during the night).

FELLOW TRAVELERS—Beginners and more experienced women who want to learn the skills of wilderness travel.

FITNESS LEVEL—Since all backpack trips are to some extent strenuous, you owe it to yourself, as well as to the group, to get into the best possible physical condition. You should have leg strength; be able to lift yourself and your pack the equivalent of two stairs at a time.

PRICE—$395. Airfare is not included.

The Spiritual Center of America
Programs for Women
PO Box 2808
Boone, NC 28607
(800) 877-77-BLISS (772-5477)
www.spiritual-center.org

This organization offers women the opportunity to experience two- to six-day retreats. The retreats are a time of deep rest and rejuvenation. The Center offers instruction in the Transcendental Meditation technique, which they say is a simple, natural technique for enlivening bliss, developing full creative potential, and dissolving accumulated stress. They say that over 4,000 women have participated in their programs, and enjoy the benefits of deep rest and rejuvenation long after they have returned home.

WHERE—They are located atop the eastern continental divide at 4,000 feet in the Blue Ridge Mountains of North Carolina, between the town of Blowing Rock and Boone.

MEALS AND ACCOMMODATIONS—All meals are included. The strictly vegetarian fare includes a wide variety of international dishes. Your accommodations are comfortable rooms overlooking Lake Shandelee.

PRICE—$320 for two days for a single occupancy with a private bath.

8

Tours for You and Your Kids

One touch of nature makes the whole world kin.
—Shakespeare

If you're a mom, grandmother, or aunt, or otherwise fortunate enough to have a child in your life, taking a vacation with that special young person can create wonderful lifetime memories for both of you. Children are fun, they're innovative, they're open to new experiences. Seeing things through the eyes of the young is a special treat. Members of the younger generation view the world and all its wonders as personal gifts to be explored and savored; unfamiliar places and people are exciting treasures. Adults can't help but feel their enchantment . . . it's contagious. Nothing escapes the curious eyes of those who are just discovering the world. They see things you might miss. Their reactions and discoveries add a new dimension to traveling.

Younger children and teens alike are also great ambassadors. It's easy for them to make friends along the way for both of you. Another bonus of traveling with a child of any age is that it enriches the bond between you. You're each other's captive audience . . . what better way to build cherished memories?

Today, there are many vacations geared especially to taking kids. There's something for each of you, as well as plenty of time to appreciate the destination together.

Wildland Adventures
3516 NE 155th St.
Seattle, WA 98155
(800) 345-4453
www.wildland.com

This organization offers authentic cultural and natural history explorations in Cost Rica, Panama, Belize, East Africa, and Peru for families with older children. In Costa Rica, the company also offers carefully planned family itineraries, distinguished by the ages of the kids and the ease of travel. Costa Rica is a great choice for family trips. A springlike climate is ideal for travel year-round. Located between two continents and two seas, Costa Rica contains astonishingly diverse and abundant tropical flora and fauna. It is a land filled with white-water rivers and waterfalls, tropical rain forests, active volcanos, cloud forests, and coral reefs. Rare and exotic wildlife abound.

The company's Temptress Family Adventure Programs take place aboard a floating hotel with many special features and options just for kids, including supervised children's beach activities, separate nature briefings geared toward the younger audience, nature journal writing, coloring and essay contests, safe, supervised water games, sea kayaking for teens, and a kids menu with an early children's dinnertime so you can dine with other adults. During summer family programs, an experienced on-board activities coordinator arranges fun and educational play for kids throughout the day and evening, including your dinner hour. Nature programs and family movies in the ship's lounge provide quiet time after a full day outdoors. Even infants can be accommodated.

The company promises that your kids will learn to love to travel, and to love learning while they travel. Special predeparture packets are prepared for young travelers to Costa Rica, including a colorful rain forest poster, a personal diary, a Spanish language book, and more.

Easter Cloud Voyage—Costa Rica (eight days)

This trip takes you aboard the M/V *Temptress Explorer* to view tropical beaches, rain forests, and national parks along the Pacific Coast of Costa Rica. This is an ideal trip for any family looking for fun and adventure that includes naturalist hikes, beaches, village visits, snorkeling (or scuba), fishing and sea kayaking, along with the amenities of an informal, mid-size ship. The *Temptress* provides access to some of the most remote and pristine beaches in Costa Rica. There are plenty of large, colorful birds, monkeys, and other wildlife in these rain forests to excite kids on easy nature walks. Highlights include a visit to the Curu Biological Reserve, a dry tropical forest where you see iguanas, monkeys, and Great Frigate birds. Scenic beaches are ideal for swimming and snorkeling.

You also stop at Cano Island, ringed with turquoise waters and coral-covered rocky reefs teeming with brilliantly colored tropical fish. Here you venture through the jungle and examine pre-Colombian artifacts and stone spheres whose origins are still a mystery. You also explore the rain forests, rivers, waterfalls, and pristine beaches of Corcovado National Park , a vast protected area with an abundance of endangered wildlife, including tree sloths, four species of monkeys, and over three hundred species of birds. Golfo Dulce is a huge protected bay in southern Costa Rica where you enjoy a tranquil afternoon on a secluded eight-hundred-acre palm-lined beach situated at the foot of the rain forest, where toucans and monkeys cavort in the trees overhead. You also have an opportunity to paddle up the Aguijitas River in a kayak, or enjoy snorkeling, swimming, and sunbathing. Another stop is Manual Antonia, one of Costa Rica's most beautiful national parks. You can hike through its open forest trails watching for squirrel, spider, and white-faced monkeys, iguanas, and many birds.

MEALS AND ACCOMMODATIONS—All meals are included. Self-service snacks are available around the clock. The 185-foot *Temptress Explorer* accommodates ninety-nine passengers. Cabins have twin single beds or one double bed, a private bathroom, individual A/C controls, and a large panoramic window. Triple rooms are also available.

FELLOW TRAVELERS—This trip tends to draw parents (including solo moms and dads) with younger children, twelve years and under, as well as grandparents.

PRICES—$1,695 for each adult; $847.50 for each child under twelve sharing a cabin with an adult; $1,271.25 for each child between twelve and seventeen during the summer months. Airfare is not included.

Monteverde Family Adventure in Costa Rica (nine days)

This is a wonderful trip for the entire family. It visits the Arenal Volcano, the Monteverde Cloud Forest Reserve, and Manuel Antonio National Park. A naturalist guide accompanies the group during the Arenal-Monteverde portion of the trip. The Monteverde Cloud Forest Reserve is a private reserve, home of the Resplendent Quetzal, one of the most beautiful birds in the Americas. The Manuel Antonio National Park is a lowland tropical rain forest, so kids get to experience different ecosystems; it is located around an active volcano, which on a clear day steams and rumbles.

MEALS AND ACCOMMODATIONS—Most meals are included. You stay in three- to four-star hotels suited for families.

FELLOW TRAVELERS—Families and single parents with children.

PRICES—$1,250 for an adult; $935 for children nine to twelve; $595 for children five to eight. Airfare is not included.

River Odysseys West
P.O. Box 579
Coeur d'Alene, ID 3816-0579
(800) 451-6034
www.rowinc.com

River rafting is this company's speciality. Other types of trips include walking, yachting, and barging. (We have included the company's adult trips in chapter 8, "Action and Adventure Tours.") ROW also offers family river adventures. A river trip is a fantastic family bonding experience: You get to play together as well as have time for each of you to pursue your own interests. On its family-focus trips, the tour stops a little more often than it does on open-enrollment trips, to allow children to run around and play. There is also an opportunity to swim (with a life jacket on) from the rafts during the calm stretches. This keeps kids from getting restless, bored, or feeling too confined.

Each day the raft floats for five or six hours; during the remainder of the day you can choose to go on short hikes or relax at the camp. Each day one of the guides serves as "family guide," leading a variety of fun-filled games. They take oar-powered rafts, paddle rafts, and inflatable kayaks on the trips, allowing everyone to find either a challenging level of activity (kayaks or paddle rafts) or a place to sit back and enjoy the scenery (oar rafts). Generally, younger children ride in the larger oar rafts with the guide rowing, but there are stretches of the river where they can share the fun of paddle rafting. Teenagers will also enjoy a go in the "duckies," which are stable inflatable kayaks.

WHERE—Along the Salmon River, Idaho.

MEALS AND ACCOMMODATIONS—All meals are included. Each evening there are two seatings for dinner. The first, at 6:00 P.M., features a menu more suitable to kids' tastes. At 7:30 P.M. a fantastic adult menu is served. Children are welcome to eat at either or both meals. Camp tents are set up by guides.

Salmon River Canyons Trip (five days)

Every summer River Odysseys West offers three or four trips on the Salmon River Canyons exclusively for families. While most of the rivers the company runs are suitable for families, this is the trip it most highly recommends for such customers. The Salmon River flows through deep canyons with spectacular scenery. The rapids are fun, yet very approachable. Camps are set on expansive white sand beaches and each has a perfect swimming hole. The dramatic scenery, warm swimming water, hot summer weather, and wilderness qualities of the area make for a perfect family vacation.

The trip begins near Whitebird, Idaho, where you have a choice of traveling on the river in three different vessels: an oar boat, on which the guide does all the work; a paddle boat, on which the guide and passengers paddle; or a "daring duckie," which is an inflatable kayak holding one or two people. You then float fifty-two miles to the confluence with the Snake River.

You continue floating another twenty-one miles on the Snake through the lower end of Hells Canyon, for a total of seventy-three miles. Along the way there's plenty of time for hiking, volleyball, enjoying the sun, fishing, and relaxing on the river. There are short hikes to visit historic sites of the Nez Percé Indians and nine-teenth-century mines.

WHERE—Idaho. Trips run July through September.

MEALS AND ACCOMMODATIONS—All meals are included. ROW guides are experts at preparing bountiful, fresh, healthy meals. In the evening camp, hors d'oeuvres are served at camp with complimentary beer and wine. Drinks are provided throughout the day. Campsites are set up by guides.

FELLOW TRAVELERS—Generally there are three to five families on a trip, so that young rafters have plenty of playmates. Some trips may have kids older than fourteen, whose interests are obviously different than those of younger children. It's a good idea to try to schedule a trip that will include children around the same age as your children.

PRICE—$1,162 to $1,265 for an adult; $995 to $1,075 for a child (depending on the time of year). Airfare is not included.

Radisson Cable Beach Resort
(Located on Cable Beach, Nassau, in the Bahamas)
Represented by Resort Marketing, Inc.
19495 Biscayne Blvd., Suite 801
Aventura, FL 33180-2321
(800) 333-3333

This group's all-inclusive vacation features spacious accommodations and all meals at the resort's six restaurants. Also included are unlimited greens fees on the resort's eighteen-hole championship golf course, snorkeling, introductory scuba lessons, and nonmotorized water sports, volleyball, table tennis, island bicycle tours, and use of the fully equipped fitness center featuring tennis courts, squash, and racquetball. In addition there are many other special activities each day as well as nightly entertainment. Also included is enrollment for children ages three to twelve in Camp Junkanoo, a supervised activities program. The camp offers a half or full day of supervised play, field trips, beach games, kids' movies, and interactive video and arcade games.

WHERE—The resort is only ten minutes from the island's international airport and colorful downtown Nassau. It is also conveniently located near many other major attractions.

MEALS AND ACCOMMODATIONS—The hotel offers a wide variety of dining options at six on-property restaurants, including Italian, Californian, "Floribbean," Bahamian, and Mexican cuisine, as well as an outdoor restaurant nestled between the beach and the picturesque tropical waterscape. There are seven hundred spacious guest rooms. Each air-conditioned room offers direct-dial telephone, cable television with in-room movies, a minibar, an in-room safe, and a private, oversize balcony with views of the ocean or the lush, tropical lagoons. Complimentary cribs are available.

FELLOW TRAVELERS—Families of all types, including solo moms and dads.

PRICES—$228 to $413 for single occupancy (depending on the season and the type of room). Children stay free in the room, with a maximum of two children per room. Baby-sitting is available at a nominal charge.

Tauck Tours, Inc.
276 Post Road West
Westport, CT 06881
(800) 468-2825
www.tauck.com

As part of their extensive escorted tour packages, this tour company has innovative "heli-hiking" adventure programs which are very popular with families. Heli-hiking, which involves bringing tourists by helicopter to remote hiking locations, was developed in 1978 as a means for summertime travelers to explore the vast untouched areas of the Canadian Rockies wilderness that lies beyond the reach of the highway—which is as close as most people ever get to the magnificent mountains themselves. The Bugaboo, Cariboo, and Bobbie Burns Lodges were built atop the mountains at approximately 3,600 feet, to house visitors to the area. Tauck uses twelve-passenger helicopters for transportation to the areas.

WHERE—The United States and Canada, Europe, Australia and New Zealand, China and Southeast Asia, Central America, Costa Rica, and South America.

FELLOW TRAVELERS—On the average group tour there are about forty participants, with a mixture of couples and singles, younger and older people, and children of all ages.

Price—$1,000 to $5,890 for double occupancy; single supplement is very variable. Airfare is not included.

Canadian Rockies Plus Bugaboo by Helicopter (eight days)

This trip is ideal for travelers with young children as well as teens, who want to see famous sights and experience a little alpine adventure. Participants will spend five days exploring Calgary, Banff, and Lake Louise and riding the Icefields Parkway, which is surely the most scenic drive in North America. Banff is a storybook village surrounded by some of the most magnificent scenery in North America.

Three days are spent heli-hiking. Each day a helicopter lifts you onto a world of glaciers, forests, snow fields, and alpine meadows. This is an alpine world that without a helicopter would take you days to reach. Every time you step off the helicopter there is something new to experience.

Guided walks and hikes are within high alpine meadows, watered by melting snows and dotted with patches of bluebells, mountain alder, cotton grass, and Indian paintbrush. Some walks may be on rocky escarpments surrounded by waterfalls and panoramic views, while others are on the glacier's surface, which occasionally rumbles as it moves along at a very fast rate. Your guides are always with you. At the end of the day you return to the lodge where you can relax in the sauna and whirlpool, or have a massage.

One of the nicest things about this trip is that although you and the youngster with you both enjoy the wonders of this spectacular area, each of you can do it at your own pace. Different levels of activity are available. Participants are divided into five different levels of interest and dexterity, running the gamut from people who do extensive hiking and are in good physical condition, to people who enjoy some light hiking but are more focused on taking pictures or learning about geology (this latter group includes the majority of the participants), to those who do little, if any, walking and remain with a guide close to the areas where they are dropped off.

MEALS AND ACCOMMODATIONS—Nineteen meals are included. Accommodations include one night at the Banff Springs Hotel, one night at the Chateau Lake Louise, one night at the Springs at Radium Golf Resort, three nights at the Bugaboo Lodge, and one night at the Westin Calgary. Chateau Lake Louise and the Banff Springs Hotel, both originally built during the late 1800s at superb locations, are the most prestigious hotels in the Canadian Rockies.

FELLOW TRAVELERS—Singles, couples, and families; people of all ages. It is not uncommon to have an eight-year-old child and an eighty-year-old grandmother enjoying this vacation together, but at different levels of activity.

PRICES—$2,390 to $2,540 per person (including children) for double occupancy; $2,145 to $2,295 for triple accommodations. Airfare is not included.

Latigo Ranch
PO Box 237
Kremmling, CO 80459
(800) 227-9655
www.latigotrails.com

Both adults and kids are catered to at this ranch. For kids there is a fully supervised children's program. Counselors teach them to ride and show them the sights on horseback. In between rides the kids swim in the heated pool, play games, explore, hike, and learn how to fish for trout in a stocked pond. They have a special program for "little buckaroos," three to five years old. Of course, if you wish to spend time with your child, they help you do that.

Adults can ride through forests of pine and aspen. Each guest is paired with one of the ranch's sixty horses for the duration of their stay. Guests are taken out for two rides each day, lasting from one and a half to two and a half hours. You can ride as often or as little as you like. Individual instruction is available in the arena just about every day. Throughout your stay the ranch gears both the rides and instruction to your level. Those who just want to admire the scenery may take the ride at a walk, while the more adventurous can enjoy rides that trot and lope. Certified arena instruction helps you enhance your riding skills. Natural horsemanship lessons are offered to help experienced riders rise to a new level of communication with their horse.

You can also help round up the cattle and learn the basics of sorting cattle from horseback in an arena event called team penning.

The Latigo Social Club serves as the hub for many activities, such as weekly western dances, and it has a pool table, Ping-Pong table, hot tub, and swimming pool. There's also a library for those who seek quiet time. For fishing enthusiasts there are streams, rivers, and ponds in the area filled with rainbow, brook, brown, and cutthroat trout.

WHERE—The ranch is located high in the spectacular Colorado Rockies at about 9,000 feet above sea level in an environment of vast heavy pine and spruce forests.

MEALS AND ACCOMMODATIONS—All meals are included. If you have dietary restrictions they will try to accommodate you. Cabins are modern log structures, fully carpeted, and have electric heat. Single-bedroom and three-bedroom units are available, each with a sitting room and fireplace or wood-burning stove. There are no phones or televisions.

FELLOW TRAVELERS—Singles, couples, and kids.

PRICES—$1,695 per week for adults; $1,120 per week for children ages six to thirteen; $825 per week for children ages three to five. Infants two and under stay free.

Hidden Creek Ranch
7600 East Blue Lake Road
Harrison, ID 83833
(208) 689-3209
www.hiddencreek.com

The mission of the owners of this ranch is to share their love for horseback riding and the great outdoors with their guests. Their six-day program offers activities scheduled throughout each day. You can do as much or as little as you desire. A full children's program is available from mid-June through August for children ages three to teens. This program includes daily horseback riding and encourages an awareness of nature and the wonder of life. Children six years and up can join the kids' mountain trail rides, while the "little dudes" will enjoy horseback riding in the ranch valley. Adult riding activities include centered riding instruction, daily horseback ride, scenic fast and challenging trail ride, all-day ride, lunch ride, champagne brunch ride, dinner ride, horse grooming and saddling lesson, hay wagon ride, cow-herding games, and barrel-racing rodeo. Additional recreational activities include fly-fishing instruction, hiking, jogging, nature walks, and more. Massages, reflexology, yoga, breathing and relaxation training, and much more is also available. In addition, there are special after-dinner activities. Winter programs are also available.

WHERE—The ranch is located in northwestern Idaho near the Coeur d'Alene Lake system in the Idaho Panhandle. It is in the heart of Idaho's "Big Water Mountain Land," at an elevation of 2,400 feet, and is surrounded by over 350 square miles of national forests.

MEALS AND ACCOMMODATIONS—All meals are included. Vegetarian, low-fat/low-cholesterol diets, food allergies, and diabetics are all catered to. Lodgings are in luxurious cabins with modern log furniture, decorated with a Native American motif, and all have a view overlooking the valley and mountains.

FELLOW TRAVELERS—Families, solo moms and dads, and kids of all ages.

PRICES—$1,969 (June, July, August) per adult, $1,615 per child, for six days, based on double occupancy.

Radisson Suite Resort on Sand Key
1201 Gulf Blvd.
Clearwater Beach, FL 34630
(800) 333-3333
www.radisson.com

This resort is a great place for family vacation fun in Florida. It offers suite accommodations, a quality children's program, and an exceptional array of amenities and services. A full-time children's and teens' activity program is directed by a professional recreation staff. Free activities called Kokomos Kids Activity Time are organized in the mornings for children ages four to twelve, while afternoon poolside sessions may require a nominal fee.

For unstructured family time, the resort's outdoor recreation area maintains an oversize, free-form swimming pool as well as a kiddie pool. You can also rent bicycles or jet skis or go water skiing. Those who desire a slower pace can just relax poolside and absorb the daily entertainment. The resort also offers a fitness center with spa, sauna, massage therapy, and three lounges. There are twenty boardwalk shops and boutiques.

WHERE—The resort is located on seven acres on Florida's west coast. It is close to Tampa Bay attractions, and central Florida day trips are only a ninety-minute drive.

MEALS AND ACCOMMODATIONS—There are 220 two-room suites and five restaurants. Each suite includes a microwave, wet bar, combined minibar-refrigerator, two televisions, entertainment center, coffeemaker, and private balcony with a view of both the Gulf of Mexico and Clearwater Bay. Meals are not included.

FELLOW TRAVELERS—People and children of all ages, from all over the United States and abroad.

PRICES—$1,259 to $1,569 for an eight-day, seven-night package. This includes a deluxe two-room suite, supervised children's activity in Lisa's Klubhouse each morning, $100 credit for in-suite dining or food and beverage at Kokomos, the Harbor Grille, or the Harbor Lounge, four tickets for the Dolphin Encounter boat cruise, a sunset trolley ride, and complimentary valet parking. For four days, three nights the cost is $599 to $699 per person for the same inclusive package. The only change is that there is a $50 food credit.

Grandtravel
6900 Wisconsin Ave., Suite 706
Chevy Chase, MD 20815
(800) 247-7651
www.grandtrvl.com

This organization offers trips for grandparents and their grandchildren to please both generations. Tours are escorted by teachers.

WHERE—Just about anywhere in the world. Each itinerary is designed to appeal to both generations. They include lots of fun-filled activities. They give special attention to natural attractions (glaciers, jungles, mountains, canyons), historical sites (native villages, ancient cities, medieval castles) and places of current interest (museums, industries, cultural attractions, and beaches).

PRICE—$4,000 to $9,000 per person. Airfare is not included.

Western Parks, Western Space (ten days)

The Old West comes alive on this trip to the Big Sky Country. Grandparents and grandchildren learn all about the cowboys, Native Americans, pioneer women, and mountain men who make up the story of the American West. The trip begins with your arrival in Rapid City, South Dakota. From here you head into the Black Hills, stopping at Mt. Rushmore National Monument. Among other impressive stops is the Devil's Tower National Monument, which rises 864 feet above the plains. Then you head north to Montana for a tour of the famous Little Bighorn Battlefield where Custer met his fate against the Lakota and Cheyenne.

Another visit is to Diamond Tail Ranch for an informative look at what real working cowboys do all day. There is also a stop at the Buffalo Bill Historical Center and then it's on to Yellowstone National Park with all its wonderful attractions, including the famous geyser Old Faithful. You then depart for the Grand Teton National Park and your hotel in Jackson Hole with all its attractions, including marvelous shops and galleries. After a farewell dinner you are transported to the Jackson Hole airport for your trip home.

MEALS AND ACCOMMODATIONS—Included in this trip are nine breakfasts, eight lunches, nine dinners, and snacks. Hotels are either deluxe, first class, or the best available.

FELLOW TRAVELERS—Grandparents and grandchildren of all ages.

PRICE—$3,995 for double occupancy; $3,830 for triple occupancy; and $3,715 for quadruple occupancy. Airfare is not included.

Space Adventures Ltd.
4718 N. 24th St.
Arlington, VA 22207
(888) 85-SPACE (857-7223)
www.spaceadventures.com

This company is on the forefront of futuristic space tourism. (For more information on the company's tours for adults see chapter 9, "Action and Adventure Tours.") For families with children there is a weekend program called the Skywatcher's Inn, which allows families to observe the stars in some of the darkest skies in the United States and the world.

WHERE—Benson, Arizona.

PROGRAM ITINERARY—You arrive at the Skywatcher's Inn, which houses an observatory, planetarium, small science museum, multimedia room, and two porches with spectacular views of the sunset and sunrise. At 3,800 feet elevation, the twenty-by-twenty-seven-foot sliding roof observatory is an ideal place to tour the night sky with six on-site telescopes. Guests meet on the porch for a southwestern-style cookout. Afterward, the entire family participates in a three- to four-hour hands-on introduction to astronomical observation under the leadership of an expert astronomer.

The following day is one of exploration. In the morning you enjoy the inn's collections of meteorites, fossils, and other scientific materials. You can then spend the afternoon in the planetarium and continue to acquaint yourself with the skies. There also is a large astronomical library and video collection. Videos can be viewed on the big-screen TV in the inn's family room. After dinner, there are guided sessions in the observatory in advanced observing. The evening concludes with the use of a twenty-inch Maksutov telescope. Last, but not least, there is a marshmallow roast under the magnificent star-filled Arizona sky. You check out after breakfast the following day.

You may wish to further explore the region's other activities, such as sight-seeing, hiking, fishing, boating, and horseback riding.

MEALS AND ACCOMMODATIONS—The package includes dinner on the first night and breakfast on the second and third days. You stay for two nights at the Skywatcher's Inn, and have access to all telescopes and facilities.

FELLOW TRAVELERS—This adventure is limited to four families, with children of all ages.

PRICE—$259 per person for double occupancy. Airfare is not included.

Kid-friendly vacations have come a long way indeed since the time when the only option was to go to Disneyland. More and more, the travel industry is recognizing the need for parents and kids to have adventures and special time together in an environment where wonderful memories are forged. So forget about asking Grandma to watch your kids: Take Grandma with you and have a great time one and all!

9

Action and
Adventure Tours

Adventure is worthwhile.—Amelia Earhart

"Exciting, exhilarating, exotic." That's how women who opt for an action-filled vacation describe their adventure. Surprises galore await travelers who seek thrilling, out-of-the-ordinary journeys. Today, more and more women are pursuing trips brimming with excitement and glamour. Women are choosing to immerse themselves in high-energy trips that are filled with new discoveries. They're joining the throngs of travelers in pursuit of adventure who are making news.

According to the Travel Industry of America, one half of U.S. adults, or seventy-four million people, have taken an adventure vacation in the last five years. More than half opted for light-adventure vacations, like cycling and yachting, but thirty-one million people engaged in hard-adventure activities like white-water rafting and scuba diving.

From beginning to end, an action-adventure vacation is a very special experience. Active exploration in the great outdoors affords a wonderful opportunity to take home memories of cultural interchanges with the local people you're bound to meet. Ambling along strange new roads, pedaling your way up picturesque hill and mountain paths, rafting rivers, or riding on an animal's back, going where no car, bus, or train can go affords an up-close-and-personal experience that you will treasure all your life. All your senses are stimulated to a more heightened awareness when you choose an adventure-packed vacation. And now, believe it or not, you may soon be able to experience the ultimate in adventure . . . going off into outer space, or at the very least, engaging in an adventure program that allows you to experience weightlessness! Read on and discover many of the exciting action and adventure tours that are available today.

Asia Tours and Travel
9888 E. Vassar Dr., Suite #204
Denver, CO 80231
(800) 543-1171

This tour operation offers unique adventures including treks, white-water rafting, and camel safaris.

WHERE—South Asia, including India, Nepal, Tibet, Pakistan, Bhutan, Vietnam, Thailand, Burma, Cambodia, and Loas.

PRICE—$1,000 to $4,500 for double occupancy; single supplement, $115 to $500. Airfare is not included.

Rajasthan Camel Safari in India: The Marwar Trail (sixteen days)

This enchanting journey through history takes you on a mounted camel safari in western Rajasthan. The tour starts with your arrival in Delhi. From there you take the train to Bikaner where the safari begins. You spend seven days living like nomads from an ancient time in the Thar desert of Rajasthan, which, unlike many deserts of the world, has an abundance of easily visible flora and fauna. Traveling in a caravan for five hours each day you can ride on a camel's back or in a camel-drawn cart. Evenings are spent by the campfire enjoying enchanting folk music and dance. Along the way you visit Indian villages where you see how the people in the area really live.

The safari ends in the desert fortress town of Jaisalmer, known as the Golden City. You have ample time to explore this incomparably romantic and unspoiled place. Then it's on to Jodhpur, the second largest city in Rajasthan, situated on the edge of the Thar Desert. The journey comes to an end with a flight to Delhi and a day of sight-seeing in the capital of India.

MEALS AND ACCOMMODATIONS—All meals are included. Cooks trained in Western cooking and hygiene are brought on the safari. Sleeping quarters on safari are "five-star tents." Amenities include carpets on the floor and bathrooms with showers. Some are permanent tents. Hotels are five-star.

FELLOW TRAVELERS—This tour accommodates no more than ten people. Usually 60 percent of the travelers are solo travelers, and the remaining 40 percent tend to be friends traveling together. In the past, mostly men took this adventure tour, but the trend is shifting, and professional women in the forty-five to fifty-five age range are now signing up for this adventure.

FITNESS LEVEL—You should be in fairly good physical shape, and it's nice if you're able to sit on a camel's back, if you wish. (You may be a bit sore at the end of your journey, but that's just part of the fun.)

PRICE—$2,390 for double occupancy; single supplement, $400. (Prices may vary slightly according to the departure date). Airfare is not included.

Bike Riders Tours
PO Box 130254
Boston, MA 02113
(800) 473-7040
www.bikeriderstours.com

This organization solely offers biking tours.

WHERE—New England states, Canada, Europe.

PRICES—$1,060 (five-day tour) to $2,990 (eight-day tour) for double occupancy; single supplement, $280 to $500. Airfare is not included.

Burgundy Luxury Bicycling Tour (seven days)

Participants bike through the vineyards of this celebrated French wine-producing region. Your ride takes you through verdant hillsides dotted with quaint stone villages and majestic chateaux. You see a rural France that has little changed over the last few centuries. The following days are spent exploring this famous area, including such delightful villages as Pouilly-Fuisse, Brancion, and Beaune, as well as a visit to Cluny, the center of medieval monasticism. Ample time is also given to exploring castle ruins and other points of interest, including renowned wine cellars where you can sample fine wines.

Each day's pedaling starts at approximately 9:00 A.M. and you continue for six to eight hours, covering from fifteen to thirty-five miles each day with one day's riding up to forty-five miles.

MEALS AND ACCOMMODATIONS—All breakfasts except one, one picnic lunch, and all dinners except one (in Beaune) are included. You savor the best food and wine of the area from the finest restaurants, where the mode of dress is casually elegant. You stay at charming hotels, châteaux, and inns chosen for their character, comfort, and location.

FELLOW TRAVELERS—The tour is limited to sixteen people. Ages range from the twenties to seventies with the majority somewhere in the middle. There is a mixture of singles (about 80 percent women) and couples.

FITNESS LEVEL—These are tours, not races. You should be fit enough to comfortably pedal up a few hills. There is plenty of time to complete the day's itinerary at your own pace. You bike fifteen to thirty-five miles each day. For those who want a more challenging route, the guide supplies information on side trips.

PRICE—$2,580 per person for double occupancy; single supplement, $450. Bike rental costs $150, or you can bring your own bike. Airfare is not included.

Country Walkers
PO Box 180
Waterbury, VT 05676
(800) 464-9255
www.countrywalkers.com

This company offers 41 walking tours around the world, ranging from four to twelve miles a day, with several choices usually offered. A walk before breakfast may be offered to capture sunrises, birds singing, or villagers opening their market. Some tours include options such as horseback riding and snorkeling.

WHERE—Europe, Central South America, Asia, Africa, the South Pacific, the United States, and Canada.

PRICE—$1,898 to $5,998 per person for double occupancy; single supplement, $200 to $1,059. Airfare is not included.

Hawaii Mythical Maui (seven days)

This is a wonderful walking tour in remote areas of Maui. Walks are punctuated by swimming from sparkling beaches, wine tasting, snorkeling, and all the other recreations offered by this gorgeous island that, according to legend, was fished up from the bottom of the sea by a giant demigod named Maui.

Your walk starts with the road to Hana where one-lane bridges pass some of the most remarkable scenery in the world. Walking continues on the black sands of Kings Highway Coastal Lava Trail to an ancient temple and the hala groves of Waianapanapa. You visit Kauiki Hill, cave birthplace of a Hawaiian queen. You walk through a bamboo forest and crane your neck to see the tops of two towering waterfalls: Makahilu (two hundred feet) and

Waimoku (four hundred feet). You also get to see Haleakala, the largest dormant volcano on the planet.

At the end of each day you can pursue the activity of your choice, including kayaking, body surfing, snorkeling in a natural jacuzzi, horseback riding, or relaxing under the trained hands of a masseuse.

MEALS AND ACCOMMODATIONS—All meals are included except one lunch. The tour operators say they seek out the gastronomic riches of the region. For the first three days you will stay at a small (eighteen units) hotel beachfront condominium on Hani Bay; during the remainder of the trip your accommodations are at a unique Hawaiian guest ranch in Kula.

FELLOW TRAVELERS—Participants are from thirty to seventy-five years old, with a mixture of couples, solo women, and single women traveling together. There are never more than eighteen people in a group with two guides.

FITNESS LEVEL—You have to be able to walk an easy to moderate terrain and average four to eight miles per day, with shorter and longer options most days.

PRICE—$2,998 per person for double occupancy; single supplement, $595. Airfare is not included. Prices may vary according to dates. If you wish to avoid the single supplement, the company will assign you a roommate. If you sign up more than ninety days prior to the trip to share a room, you will not be required to pay the single supplement fee if the company cannot find you a roommate.

Tre Laghi
1500 S.W. 5th Ave.—Suite 2506
Portland, OR 97201
(800) 293-1117
www.trelaghi.com

This tour company offers luxury walking tours that are designed to highlight specific areas of a country and are best enjoyed at a slower and more relaxed pace. Walking along country lanes and trails, participants explore areas seldom visited by tourists, meeting the townspeople and sampling local foods and wines.

The tours allow for flexibility in choosing your daily activities. Each day a guided excursion is offered that covers between six and ten miles, but you can enjoy each day's outing at your own pace.

WHERE—Italy, Switzerland, and France

PRICE—$1,900 to $3,380 per person for double occupancy; single supplement, $275 to $385. Airfare is not included.

Exploring the Swiss/Italian Lake District (eight days)

This tour emphasizes the Swiss/Italian lake district's varied and natural beauty. Your trip begins in Lugano, Switzerland. A cable car takes you up to the village of Bre high above Lugano where you explore this majestic alpine landscape. The following day you travel by private boat across Lake Lugano into Italy. You begin walking from the small town of Porlezza to Lake Como and then through pine forests to the hillside village of Bene Lario. From here you continue on to Cardano and Loveno. You also visit the charming lakeside towns of Bellagio and Menaggio. For those who may like to hike higher above the lake, there is a departure from Tremezzo for a journey to the sanctuary of St. Martino, which rests on a rock ledge high above Menaggio and provides a stunning view of the central lake region. A boat then takes you to the charming fishing village of Varenna. The tour continues with a forty-minute hydrofoil ride to Como. Afterward you travel to the town of Cernobbio. Your adventure continues with a cable-car ride to Brunate, high above Como, where you follow the meandering forest-and-meadow trail down to the waterside village of Torno. Your last morning is in Como only one hour away from the Milan airport.

MEALS AND ACCOMMODATIONS—All breakfasts and lunches and six dinners are included. Gourmet meals including specialities of the region and wine are served. You spend at least two nights in various deluxe hotels.

FELLOW TRAVELERS—A group usually consists of twelve to fourteen people, both couples and single men and women. Their ages usually range from forty to seventy-five, with the majority in their late forties and fifties.

FITNESS LEVEL—You should enjoy being outdoors all day and trust in your feet. At points with a more challenging walk, there is always an alternative for those who prefer a more relaxed itinerary.

PRICE—$3,380 per person for double occupancy; single supplement, $320. Airfare is not included.

River Odysseys West/Remote Odysseys Worldwide
PO Box 579
Coeur d'Alene, ID 83816
(800) 451-6034

Wilderness river rafting is this company's speciality. It also offers walking tours, yachting, and barging trips. The guides (both men and women) are talented boatmen and boatwomen whose primary responsibility is to get you safely down the river. Beyond this they are fantastic storytellers.

WHERE—River rafting and walking tours in Idaho, the state known for having more white-water river miles than any other in the nation, over 3,000 miles in all. Their other trips include:

- Rain-forest rafting on Ecuador's Rio Upano in the Amazon basin.
- Yachting along Turkey's Mediterranean Coast or Croatia's Dalmatian Coast.
- Barging in France.

PRICE RANGE—$790 to $1,445 per person on river trips in the United States; there is no single supplement option for tents. For hotel accommodations, the single supplement for two nights is $80 to $120. Airfare is not included.

Rafting the Middle Fork of the Salmon River in the Frank Church Wilderness Area of Idaho (six days)

Among river runners, the Middle Fork is a legend. Its 105 miles of pure, clear, free-flowing river drops 3,000 feet through the heart of the River of No Return Wilderness. This remote river is protected by Congress as one of America's first wild and scenic rivers.

Your trip begins at nearly 6,000 feet above sea level. At first, the river is narrow and shallow, but soon numerous side creeks deepen the way. The rapids are frequent and challenging. The Middle Fork River is rich in history, and there are stops where you can visit Indian rock paintings and pioneer homesteads. Hikes underneath Waterfall Creek and up to Veil Falls are highlights of the trip. Farther downstream, you enter Impassable Canyon, where you are awed by vertical granite mountains of staggering dimensions.

MEALS AND ACCOMMODATIONS—Meals are deluxe, including hot and cold hors d'oeuvres served before dinner each day. A cargo raft and guide go ahead each day and set up camp, including your tent, tables, and chairs for dining, and sun showers (bags filled with water that are heated during the day). All camping gear is provided. Everyone has his or her own tent.

FELLOW TRAVELERS—Participants are of all ages; there are singles, family groups, and couples.

FITNESS LEVEL—You just have to be in reasonably good shape.

PRICE—$1,195 to $1,585 for an adult; $1,095 to $1,395 for a youth (under sixteen). Prices vary according to dates. The tour operates June through September only. Airfare is not included.

Cross Country International
PO Box 11700
Millbrook, NY 12545
(800) 828-8768
www.equestrianvacations.com

This company offers horseback riding vacations, and it also has training vacations in cross-country jumping, stadium jumping, hunt seat equitation, basic equitation, and dressage.

WHERE—France, Italy, Spain, Ireland, Scotland, England, Costa Rica, the United States, Portugal, and Greece.

PRICE—$790 to $2,295 per person for double occupancy; not all trips have a single supplement; others vary from $25 per night to $260 per week. Airfare is not included.

Costa Rica Trail, Guanacaste, Costa Rica (five days)

This horseback riding tour in Costa Rica affords a most unusual experience through one of the world's most beautiful tropical areas. Costa Rica, the jewel of Central America, is noted for its lush vegetation, ornamental flowers such as orchids and birds-of-paradise, and unusual animals. This program takes place on the west coast of Costa Rica, along the Pacific Ocean in the sparsely populated province of Guanacaste, an area with beaches of every description (along which you will ride), mangrove trees, and breathtaking tropical forests.

You ride along the coast from beach to beach and on country roads through picturesque fishing villages. You gallop along the beach and enjoy a swim in the sea with your horse. There's also plenty of time to swim and snorkel in the Pacific Ocean and lounge on the beach or by the pool. The "Criollo" horses you ride are of mixed breeding, and most have the blood of the Spanish horses brought from the Old World by the Conquistadors in the sixteenth century.

MEALS AND ACCOMMODATIONS—All meals are included, along with four-star accommodations in beach hotels and guest houses; all have private baths and many feature views of the ocean.

FELLOW TRAVELERS—Professional people who range in age from thirty-five to sixty-five and who generally ride on the weekends; usually 60 percent are female and 40 percent male; about 60 percent are single people, and 40 percent are married couples.

PRICE—$1,545 (including horses) per person for double occupancy; single supplement, $150. Airfare is not included.

Flying A Ranch
771 Flying A Ranch Rd.
Pinedale, WY 82941
(307) 367-2385
www.flyinga.com

This is a western U.S.A. vacation for adults. Unlimited riding, guided hiking, fly-fishing with lessons and equipment, and mountain bikes are all included. Wranglers guide horseback riders through cool groves of aspen and pine to view the scenic splendor of the mountains. Fishing for spotted rainbow and brook trout is available in both of the ranch's two large stream-fed ponds, or they arrange for guides to take you off the ranch to one of the nearby mountain lakes, streams, and rivers, including the Snake, Green, and New Fork. You can walk, hike, or mountain-bike through mountain meadows to view wildlife, including deer, elk, and antelope. A social hour precedes the evening meal, and guests are encouraged to gather in the cozy lounge overlooking the ranch ponds and the mountains. There are no children's activities.

WHERE—The ranch is located about forty miles southeast of Jackson Hole, Wyoming, in a spectacular high mountain valley at 8,300 feet, surrounded by the Gros Ventre and Wind River ranges.

MEALS AND ACCOMMODATIONS—Guests are served three meals daily. Built in 1929, the ranch has great historical significance and has retained much of its original flavor and character. There are six handcrafted log cabins and the main lodge. Cabins contain private baths and kitchenettes, and most have a fireplace or wood-burning stove.

FELLOW TRAVELERS—The ranch accepts a maximum of fourteen guests. The ages range from thirties to sixties—the majority in their forties and fifties. There are both couples and singles.

PRICE—$1,675 for single occupancy. Airfare is not included.

Himalayan Travel
110 Prospect St.
Stamford, CT 06901
(800) 225-2380
www.gorp.com/himtravel.htm

This company offers escorted adventure tours in exotic lands. Many of its tours include a variety of activities, including trekking, canoeing, rafting, cycling, and sailing adventures. Its speciality is treks in the Himalayas.

WHERE—South and Central America, Africa, Europe, Middle East, and Asia, including Nepal, Tibet, India, Himalayan Peaks, Bhutan, and Kikkim.

PRICE—$600 to $5,000 for double occupancy (prices are very variable); single supplement is not always available. Roommates are provided. Airfare is not included.

Everest Adventure—Nepal (thirteen days)

This is the easiest of the treks in the Everest area. Your vacation starts in Kathmandu where you are met at the airport. Taking you through the land of the legendary Sherpas, the trek offers you stunning close-up mountain views, including Mount Everest. Each day's trek averages eight to ten miles. The first two days of your journey are given to a trek briefing and a sight-seeing tour of Kathmandu, with plenty of time to prepare for your trek and to wander around the city. The following day you fly along the Himalayan mountain chain to Lukla. You begin your slow eight-day trek along the Dudh Kosi valley from here. You walk through beautiful tracts of pine and rhododendron forest with the peaks of Thamserku and Kusum Kanguru soaring above the trail. From there it is a steep ascent to Namche Bazaar, the capital of the famous Khumbu Sherpas, where you are rewarded with spectacular mountain vistas, including the world's highest peak, Mount Everest. The trail continues to Thyangboche. Here you savor the stunning scenery, with the peaks of Everest, Lhotse, Nuptse, and Ama Dablam soaring to the top of the world. Your return journey is via the villages of Khumjung and Kunde back to the airstrip at Lukla. Returning to Kathmandu, you have time to relax, shop, or sample the delights of the many restaurants.

MEALS AND ACCOMMODATIONS—A cook accompanies the trek providing a variety of healthful meals. Evenings on the trek are spent in lodge accommodations. In Kathmandu you stay in a comfortable, centrally located, old Rana palace.

FELLOW TRAVELERS—There is usually an equal number of men and women, with ages ranging from twenties to seventies (most in their thirties and forties). Usually about 60 percent of the trekkers are single and 40 percent are couples.

FITNESS LEVEL—All treks require, at the very least, a reasonable level of fitness. This trip is rated moderate plus. The trekking may involve walking for up to seven hours over hilly terrain on well-defined trails. Altitudes will exceed 3,000 meters and sometimes reach over 5,000 meters.

PRICE—$1,325 to $1,395 (depending on the time of the year); single supplement is by special request only, $250. The company will provide a roommate. Airfare is not included.

Overseas Adventure Travel
347 Congress St.
Boston, MA 02210
(800) 955-1925
www.oattravel.com

This company offers cultural and wildlife explorations that include a lot of walking, but the pace is never exhausting. Free time is always built into the trip and participants can feel free to sit out a day or skip a particular activity.

WHERE—Europe, Asia, Africa, Australia.

PRICE—$1,490 to $4,490 for double occupancy; single supplements are very variable. If the tour operator cannot match you with a roommate, there is no charge for single accommodations. Airfare from a gateway city is included.

Machu Picchu, Peru, and the Galapagos Islands (eighteen days)

On this trip you enjoy a combination of in-depth exploration of Machu Picchu and a full week aboard a yacht with stops at fourteen remarkable destinations. Your trip begins with visits to the great colonial cities of Lima and Cuzco. From there you travel by train high into Peru's Andes mountains to Macchu Picchu where you explore this Lost City of the Incas on an overnight stay. You then fly to the Galapogos Islands. Straddling the equator 670 miles off the coast of Ecuador, the Galapogos archipelago consists of twelve major islands. Here, the mysteries of nature are very much in evidence with fascinating creatures found nowhere else on earth. For the next seven days you meander via yacht from island to island. On the island of Bartolome, you see lava formations and climb a volcanic cone. Walking through a lunar landscape, you climb to the summit of a dormant volcano for views of the famous Pinnacle Rock. There's also time for swimming and snorkling expeditions.

MEALS AND ACCOMMODATIONS—The thirty-eight meals (fifteen breakfasts, eleven lunches, twelve dinners) included provide an authentic experience of the local culture. Eight nights are spent in comfortable small hotels and lodges, and seven nights aboard a first-class eighty-three-foot-long yacht with ten double cabins. Each cabin has a private bath, a shower, and a window, and is fully air-conditioned.

FITNESS LEVEL—This trip is rated moderate/challenging. It is quite active and may include walking or hiking for several hours. You should be in good physical condition.

FELLOW TRAVELERS—Ages generally range from fifty to seventy years; 67 percent of travelers are women. There are never more than sixteen people in a group.

PRICE—$3,890 to $4,190 for double occupancy; single supplement, $490. Airfare from Miami is included.

Myths and Mountains
976 Tee Court
Incline Village, NV 89451
(800) 670-MYTH (6984)
www.mythsandmountains.com

This tour company offers educational adventures off the beaten path. Each trip focuses on one of five topics:

- Wildlife and the environment
- Folk medicine and traditional healing
- Religion and holy sites
- Learning journeys
- Cultures and crafts

WHERE—India, Chile, Ecuador, Bolivia, Peru, Tibet.

PRICE—$800 to $4,000 for double occupancy; single supplement, $200 to $500. Airfare is not included.

Peru—Weavings and Crafts of the Andes (thirteen days)

This trip explores Peru's world renowned artistic heritage. With its beautifully crafted weavings, hand-loomed rugs, wall hangings called arpilleras, cloth dolls, carved gourds, pottery, and dramatic jewelry, Peru is a craft lover's paradise. On this vacation you explore the Cuzco area and surrounding villages and visit museums and cultural institutions. A highlight of the trip is to meet with local villagers, wander through their studios and homes, learn their crafts, and actually try some of their techniques. Your guide is a native of Chinchero, a traditional Quechua community in the highlands of Peru.

Your trip begins with your arrival in Lima where you connect to a flight to Cuzco. The following day you drive over the hills of Cuzco and down into the Sacred Valley with fantastic market and craft stops along the way. Continuing on, you explore the Pisaq Inca ruins, a complex system of irrigated terraces. The next day, backpack in tow, you visit small remote villages and meet with local weavers. The following morning you catch a train to Machu Picchu for two full days of exploring one of the most sacred sites in South America. Your trip continues with more museum stops. You also leave the beaten path for a climb up to a village in one of the main valleys leading into the magnificent Vilconata Range. Here the weaving styles and mythological stories are quite different than those you have seen so far. The trip continues with more wonderful stops to see sacred ruins, weavings, and other treasures of the area.

MEALS AND ACCOMMODATIONS—All breakfasts are included, plus nine lunches and a farewell dinner. Your hotels reflect the culture of the area.

FELLOW TRAVELERS—Mostly women interested in crafts, aged thirty to sixty.

FITNESS LEVEL—This trip consists of easy to moderate walking.

PRICE—$1,687 to $2,240 depending on the number of travelers; single supplement, $373. Airfare is not included.

Boundary Country Trekking
7925 Gunflint Trail
Grand Marais, MN 55604
(800) 322-8327
www.boundarycountry.com

This company offers dogsledding trips and camping expeditions. Trips are led by an experienced dog musher who serves as your instructor and guide. Participants mush their own team twenty to thirty miles per day, one person per sled. Three- to eight- and eleven-day trips are available.

WHERE—Minnesota's Boundary Water Canoe Area. Wilderness trips are from late November through mid-March. The program is then moved to the Northwest Territories where trips are offered until April.

PRICE—$695 (two-day trip) to $3,400 (eleven-day trip). Appropriate clothing (parkas, boots, and mitts, etc.) is available for rent. Equipment provided includes sleds, sled bags, and dogs. On camping trips all camping equipment is provided. Airfare is not included.

Across the Boundary Waters Mushing Adventures (five days)

This is the company's premiere Minnesota trip of the season. Participants mush through some of the area's most beautiful and remote wilderness. The trip includes five days of mushing.

WHERE—Across the Boundary Waters, Minnesota.

MEALS AND ACCOMMODATIONS—All meals are included. Three nights are spent in cabins, one night in a yurt, and two nights in an "Arctic Oven" tent heated by wood heaters. Sleeping bags are provided at the yurts.

FELLOW TRAVELERS—Trips are limited to six participants. People of all ages from teens to seniors in their seventies, both men and women, participate. Many trips include singles.

FITNESS LEVEL—No experience is required, but you must be moderately physically fit, able to walk several miles, and have a good sense of balance. Mushing involves periods of low activity, such as riding the runners, and periods of heavy exertion, such as running uphill and physically steering the sled over and around obstacles on the trail.

PRICE—$1,735. Airfare is not included.

Natural Habitat Adventures
2945 Center Green Court—Suite H
Boulder, CO 80301
(800) 543-8917
www.nathab.com

This tour operator offers a variety of adventures including nature safaris, expedition voyages, photo adventures, wildlife workshops, and special birding expeditions.

- *Nature safaris* bring travelers in close contact with the world's greatest wildlife sites.
- *Expedition voyages* allow travelers to explore untouched areas of the world from specially designed cruising vessels.
- *Photo adventures* offer fantastic opportunities for photographers of all skills.
- *Wildlife workshops* give travelers a chance to assist scientists in performing important field research on animals and their habitats.
- *Special birding expeditions* are for those travelers who enjoy the fun of observing some of the world's greatest birds, as well as other wildlife.

WHERE—All over the globe.

PRICE—$1,995 to $5,995 for double occupancy; single supplement is very variable, from $300 and up. Airfare is not included.

Seal Watch Adventure (six days)

Every March, 250,000 harp seals enter the Gulf of St. Lawrence to bear their young on a vast floating ice field. Known as white-coats, these adorable newborn pups shed their snowy white fur and turn gray within three weeks. For hundreds of years these seals were hunted for their immaculate white fur. Now visitors can safely and comfortably spend time with these captivating animals as they enjoy peace on the ice. The journey to the herds is made via helicopter and can take between ten and forty-five minutes depending on the location of the seals. After the pilots choose a suitable ice pan, they set down a couple of hundred yards from the herd. Pilots and helicopters remain with you during your entire stay on the ice for your comfort.

When not visiting the seals, you can participate in exciting outdoor activities such as skiing, snowshoeing, and moonlight hikes.

WHERE—The Gulf of St. Lawrence and the picturesque Magdalen Islands.

MEALS AND ACCOMMODATIONS—All breakfasts and the first and final dinners are included. Participants stay at hotels (all rooms have a private bath) on the Magdalen Island near the Halifax Airport.

FITNESS LEVEL—Only a low level of physical fitness is required. For those who are not particularly agile, the staff will do whatever is necessary to make the trip comfortable. They are even prepared to guide handicapped travelers to the ice.

FELLOW TRAVELERS—Singles are encouraged to join this program. The tour operator says since the people who opt for this adventure possess a unique enthusiasm for nature that may not be shared by family and friends, many people come on the adventure alone. The oldest participant on this trip was 102 years old and the youngest was two.

PRICE—$1,995 to $3,745 (depending on how many trips to the ice you take; one to four trips are available) per person for double occupancy; single supplement, $285. Air transportation from Halifax (where the tour begins) to the Magdalen Islands is included. Airfare to Halifax is not included. Use of expedition suits and warm boots for ice trips and outdoor equipment for all outdoor activities is included.

Sierra Club Outings
85 Second St.—Second Floor
San Francisco, CA 94105
(415) 977-5522
www.sierraclub.org/outings

This organization offers 350 adventure trips to members (membership rates vary from $19 to $1,000, depending on membership category, age, and income) including cycling, camping, hiking, canoeing and kayaking, birding, backpacking, fishing, and rafting. Leaders of groups are experienced people who volunteer their time to take you to the places they love. This organization also has service trips for people who want to donate their time to various types of community service. These projects include building and maintaining trails, revegetating overused areas, assisting wildlife researchers, and mapping archaeological sites.

WHERE—The United States, Latin America, China, Canada, Africa, Europe, and Greenland.

PRICE—$165 to $4,995 for double occupancy (prices are very variable); single supplement is not always available.

Natural Treasures of Belize and Guatemala (twelve days)

You begin this tour exploring Belize, an English-speaking democracy, with an amazing variety of scenery, people, flora, and fauna. The tropical forests of this tiny country are home to more than three hundred species of birds, exotic plants, flowers, and animals. Offshore lie the turquoise waters of the Caribbean and the 150-mile-long barrier reef, second largest in the world, dotted with beautiful sandy islands called cayes. In these crystal waters are dolphins, manatees, sea turtles, ornate coral formations, and fantastically colored fish.

A short flight from Belize City takes you to neighboring Guatemala where you travel the easternmost area, El Peten, a wild, low-lying lush jungle. This least visited part of the country to tourists is home to a wondrous variety of exotic animals, particularly birds. You also explore the greatest Mayan religious center yet uncovered and the most awe-inspiring site in the whole country, the mysterious ruins of Tikal. In addition, you can enjoy hiking, swimming, snorkeling, rafting, canoeing, bird-watching, nature and archaeology study, and meeting the friendly inhabitants.

WHERE—This circle trip begins and ends in Belize City.

MEALS AND ACCOMMODATIONS—All meals are included. You stay in a waterfront hotel in Belize. At other stops you stay in rustic cabins that are eco-efficient. Each room has its own composting toilet and a shower. The water is collected rainwater, which must be used sparingly.

FELLOW TRAVELERS—There are up to fifteen people in a group. The average age is about forty-five, with a mix of couples and singles (on more vigorous trips ages often range from twenty and up).

FITNESS LEVEL—This trip is rated moderate. Hiking, walking, or swimming are almost everyday activities, so you should be in fairly good physical condition. It is not necessary to have snorkeling experience, but you should be able to swim competently in order to enjoy it.

PRICE—The cost depends on how many people are in the tour. If there are eleven or less the price is $2,645 per person for double occupancy. If there are twelve to twenty participants the price is $2,395 for double occupancy; single supplement is not available, but the tour operator will match you with a roommate. Airfare is not included.

Dolphin Camp
1654 Hamlet Chapel Road
Pittsboro, NC 27312
(800) 451-2562
www.dolphin.com

Dolphin Camp is a five-day dolphin-study vacation in Florida. Your stay includes dock time with dolphins to develop a close-up acquaintance; catamaran boat trips to meet with a special pod of wild dolphins; swims with dolphins in natural semicaptive environments; sessions with dolphin research experts on care and training, and much more.

WHERE—Florida Keys.

MEALS AND ACCOMMODATIONS—All meals are included. You stay at the Cheeca Lodge located in Islamorada, "the purple isle," in the upper keys. Cheeca is a four-star resort nestled in twenty-seven acres of lush tropical gardens.

FELLOW TRAVELERS—This vacation attracts a broad range of ages, from teens to people in their sixties; most are between twenty-five and fifty-five. A group usually consists of a maximum of thirty people, mostly single women.

PRICE—$2,195 for double occupancy (teens pay the same price; the trip is not suitable for younger children); single supplement, $425. Airfare is not included.

Space Adventures, Ltd.
4350 N. Fairfax Dr.
Arlington, VA 22203
(888) 85-SPACE (857-7223)
www.spaceadventures.com

This company offers a unique program called "Steps to Space." While the operators' ultimate goal is to take you for a ride in space, at the present time they offer a variety of space-related vacations. If you want to see a space launch up-close, or tour the world's space programs, or float in zero gravity, or look at the Russian space program, this company has a package to fulfill your fantasies.

WHERE—United States, Puerto Rico, Mexico, Machu Picchu, Russia.

PRICE—$259 per person to $98,000.

Zero-Gravity Flight Program (five days)

You can actually experience weightlessness without leaving earth. For thirty years, NASA has trained astronauts using a KC-135 parabolic flight aircraft to achieve zero-gravity. Now this tour operator has made weightless flights available to adventure tourists in Russia. This once-in-a lifetime adventure begins with your arrival in Moscow where you enjoy a tour of the city. The following day you leave Moscow for Star City and the Yuri Gagarin Training Center where you receive a brief overview of the center and its activities. You then report for health screening and receive your flight suit. A cosmonaut joins you at the center for lunch to discuss your questions about the upcoming flight and the zero-g experience.

Then it's time for the big moment! You board the Ilyushin-76 (a large, specially outfitted, training jet used by the Russian Space Agency to prepare cosmonauts for space training) and prepare for a two-hour parabolic ride you'll never forget. You experience between seven and ten minutes of weightlessness (in twenty-eight to thirty-second segments) during the flight. Your aircraft does aerobolic maneuvers at 20,000 to 30,000 feet. This is like being on a roller coaster in the sky. You leave from and return to Star City and stay in that vicinity.

Included is a post-flight tour of the facilities at Star City, where you'll visit many space simulators, You will also be introduced to several cosmonauts as they prepare for space flight.

WHERE—Star City, Russia.

MEALS AND ACCOMMODATIONS—The experience includes two nights in a hotel, an astronaut-cosmonaut cocktail reception, everything pertaining to the flight (photos, video, lunch, a genuine flight suit, all equipment usage), and transportation to and from Star City.

FELLOW TRAVELERS—This adventure appeals to space buffs, both men and women, of all ages, from people in their twenties to those in their sixties. Each group consists of ten to twelve people.

FITNESS LEVEL—You should not have any neck, back, or heart problems. You should be able to walk on a treadmill for ten minutes at a normal walking speed. Prior to participating in this program the company recommends that you be examined by a physician who can certify your health.

PRICE—$5,400 per person, based on single occupancy. Airfare to Russia is not included.

Sub-Orbital Space Flight

You will soon be able to experience the grandeur of space travel and earn astronaut status! Space Adventures is now working with leading space vehicle development companies to bring you the same, once-in-a-lifetime, history-making flight excursion experienced by Alan Shepard in 1961 when he was launched on a fifteen-minute suborbital flight. The company is currently taking reservations for flights aboard these new vehicles. Departures are being planned for late 2002/2003.

When the momentous day arrives, participants will don flight suits and board the vehicle. They will return with "astronaut status," since the United States awards that designation to anyone who flies above fifty miles in altitude. Depending on the launch vehicle chosen, participants will either blast off from the ground with the roar of rockets or depart from an airport with a jet-assisted takeoff. This breathtaking, once-in-a-lifetime flight to sixty-two miles altitude will last between thirty and ninety minutes, depending on the vehicle chosen.

FELLOW TRAVELERS—Reservations are being taken for up to one hundred people.

PRICE—$98,000. An initial deposit of $6,000 is required to reserve a seat. Proceeding payments are required in $12,000 installments every twelve months. All monies are held in an escrow account.

Concluding this chapter, we can truly say the sky is the limit in choosing an action and adventure vacation. Destinations and activities are without bounds! So let your imagination soar! The time has never been better for the solo woman traveler to stray from the usual to the exotic and experience the thrill of the extraordinary.

— 10 —

Special-Interest
Vacations

*A mind that is stretched by a new experience can
never go back to its old dimension.*
—Oliver Wendell Holmes

Are you an opera buff, a cooking or wine maven? Do you
delight in delving into the past? Have you daydreamed about
going on an archaeological jaunt? Are you fascinated with other
cultures? Do you love exploring museums and sites of antiquity?
Do you like to dabble in painting or crafts? Would you like to get
closer to your roots or make a religious pilgrimage? Whatever your
special interest, be assured there's a vacation program especially
designed to take you where you can experience it, explore it, and
enjoy it to the fullest. Going off on a holiday centered on your particular passion is a great way to meet others who share your enthusiasm. Today, there are special interest getaways dedicated to
learning and growth that are combined with the usual sorts of
vacation activities to fit all tastes. Just take your pick.

Archaeological Tours
271 Madison Ave., Suite 904
New York, NY 10016
(212) 986-3054

Tour participants are given a unique opportunity to see and understand historically important and culturally significant areas of the
world. Distinguished scholars who emphasize the historical,
anthropological, and archaeological aspects of the areas visited
accompany each tour, along with a local tour guide and an escort
from the tour operator's office.

WHERE—South America, Europe, Asia, Africa, the Middle East.

PRICE—$4,000 to $6,500 for double occupancy; single supplement,
$400 to $700. Airfare is included.

Khmer Kingdoms: Myanmar, Thailand, Laos, and Cambodia (twenty-four days)

This tour focuses on the historical, religious, and aesthetic
aspects of these four countries. It begins in Cambodia with four
days at Angkor Wat and continues to the magnificent seventh-cen-
tury Khmer temples at Wat Phou in Laos, the Khmer ruins in
remote northeastern Thailand, and ends in Myanmar (Burma)
with visits to the ancient royal cities, glittering pagodas, and golden
temples in Rangoon, Mandalay, and Pagan.

MEALS AND ACCOMMODATIONS—All meals are included. You stay in
the best available accommodations in the mainstream of local life.

FELLOW TRAVELERS—Tour participants tend to be in their forties
and up; some tours do get younger people. Many are retirees,
many are professionals. Half are usually couples and half singles,
often with equal amounts of men and women.

PRICE—$6,340 for double occupancy; single supplement, $775.
Airfare from Los Angeles and all internal flights are included.

International Council for Cultural Exchange
5 Bellport Lane
Bellport, NY 11713
(516) 286-5228

The ICCE offers cultural travel programs based on music, the arts, languages, and cultures. It is a nonprofit organization established in 1982 with the purpose of fostering international exchange programs between universities and cultural contacts between people. Upcoming getaways include opera, art and painting, music, language, and general culture trips.

WHERE—Italy, France, Eastern Europe, Russia, Scandinavia, China, Japan.

PRICE—$2,479 to $4,298 for double occupancy; single supplement, $250 to $725. Airfare from New York City is included.

Italy Opera Trip (thirteen days)

This trip offers a blend of seeing opera performances, discussions with an expert, and experiencing the culture, background, and places where opera developed. You see some of the world's greatest works performed by some of the world's greatest stars. Operas vary from year to year. In 2001, they include *Cenerentola, Rigoletto, Aida, Nabucco, Tosca,* and *Norma.* You experience the artistic, musical, and cultural riches of Italy, including stops in such cities as Milan, Verona, Venice, Florence, and Macerata. There's plenty of sight-seeing and even a day at the beach on the Italian Rivera.

MEALS AND ACCOMMODATIONS—All breakfasts and dinners are included. Accommodations are first class.

FELLOW TRAVELERS—Opera buffs, men and women, usually ranging in age from fifty to eighty from all over the United States.

PRICE—$4,398 including guided sight-seeing and opera tickets; single supplement, $725. Airfare from New York is included.

Gabriele's Travels to Italy
1610 14th St. N.W., Suite 302
Rochester, MN 55901
(888) 287-8733

The food and wine tours designed by this tour operator give travelers a real *taste* of Italian culture. Cooking classes, wine tasting, field trips to pasta and chocolate factories, wineries, cheese factories, and olive-oil mills, sight-seeing, and art/history lectures are some of the various highlights included in different tours.

WHERE—Picturesque towns in Italy.

PRICE—$1,849 to $2,900 based on double occupancy; single supplement is very variable. Airfare is not included.

La Dolce Vita (The Sweet Life) (ten days)

This tour is designed for women traveling alone. You arrive in the town of Bari where you are transferred to your hotel and enjoy a delicious get-acquainted dinner that evening. The following day is dedicated to rest and relaxation. You can indulge yourself in a massage, mud bath, or the sauna (included in the price). The next day, feeling rested and revitalized, you take a short ride to Locorotondo and Cisternino, two of the best wine-producing areas in the Apulia region. That afternoon is spent in a cooking class to learn the secrets of preparing fresh pasta. You then head to Ostuni, an ancient medieval town, and the elegant town of Martina Franca. The following day you are taken to Venosa, the home of Horace, a famous Roman philosopher. Here you will enjoy a guided tour and an overnight stay. Then you depart for Melfi, a typical southern Italian city with many monuments from different periods in history and contrasting architectural design. Your next stop is the wine-producing area of Vulture. You get to taste several of the home-made pastas produced in a unique manner in this area: lagane, fusilli, orecchiette, and maccheroni. From here you go to Matera, known for its Sassi, the ancient cave dwellers' quarters. Your last day of travel is in Matera, where you visit some of the best preserved churches dug in the rock with interesting fresco paintings. That afternoon you can engage in the annual festivities of Madonna de la Bruna. This is one of the last authentic traditions that has survived the centuries and today draws thousands of people from the surrounding communities. The day ends with a fireworks show. After breakfast the next day, you head home.

MEALS AND ACCOMMODATIONS—All meals and two glasses of wine with dinner are included. You stay at four-star hotels.

FELLOW TRAVELERS—Women of all ages, from all walks of life.

PRICE—$2,550 for single occupancy (no double occupancy is available).

Giuliano Bugialli's Foods of Italy
60 Sutton Place South
New York, NY 10022
(212) 813-9552
www.bugialli.com

Hands-on cooking lessons are given by Giuliano Bugialli, who in 1973 founded the first English-speaking cooking school in Italy. His school is now known worldwide. Week-long programs all follow a common theme: providing a well-rounded base for the study of Italian cooking. Every one of the programs is unique. Each year, new programs are added as Giuliano seeks out one or more regions of Italy and arranges an in-depth study of the customs and cooking of the areas he has carefully researched. This program is an excursion into the sights and tastes of some lesser-known parts of this beautiful country. Giuliano himself leads all trips.

WHERE—Various towns in Italy.

PRICE—$3,600 to $4,000 for double occupancy; single supplement, $700. Airfare is not included.

Cooking in Florence Program (seven days)

Giuliano recently opened a new exciting kitchen in the Chianti Classico wine and olive oil country, built into a centuries-old farmhouse just outside of Florence. Participants are transported here for classes by private bus. Classes last about four hours followed by a full lunch with appropriate wines. Giuliano teaches every class himself. Techniques are demonstrated first. When it's time to work, students choose the dishes they want to prepare from the day's varied roster of recipes, which include all the elements of Italian food. Recipes range from simple but unusual sauces for pasta to the most complex party preparation. Each day's schedule is variable with the other events of the day determining whether the cooking lesson itself begins in the morning or early afternoon and the dinner is in the city or the country, at an elegant restaurant, a rustic trattoria, or at school.

MEALS AND ACCOMMODATIONS—All meals are included. Participants stay at a modern, first-class, centrally located hotel.

FELLOW TRAVELERS—There are usually sixteen to twenty participants with a mixture of couples and singles, all ages.

PRICE—$3,600 for double occupancy; single supplement, $700. Airfare is not included.

Jane Butel's Cooking School
125 Second St. N.W.
Albuquerque, NM 87102
(800) 472-8229
www.janebutel.com

This school offers one-week and weekend classes on New Mexican and southwestern cooking. Jane Butel, a leading authority on southwestern cooking and author of sixteen southwestern cookbooks, is the lead instructor at each cooking session. Classes are taught in her state-of-the art cooking school. Students explore first-hand the intricacies of southwestern cuisine, from rolling your own tamales to preparing innovative chili pepper dishes. Butel not only teaches insider secrets to successful cooking, she also weaves in the history of southwestern food—from its beginnings in Indian Pueblo kitchens to its modern-day popularity as the second most preferred food in America.

WHERE—Albuquerque, New Mexico.

SAMPLE WEEK—The week-long class begins with a get-acquainted cocktail session followed by dinner at a restaurant specializing in New Mexican dishes. The following days unfold at 9:00 A.M. when Jane presents the menu for the day. Cooking takes place from 9:30 A.M. to 12:30 P.M. with the guidance of Jane and her staff. From 12:30 P.M. to 1:30 P.M. you enjoy a bountiful luncheon of all the dishes prepared by all the students. Afternoons you are free to take in the beauty and treasures of New Mexico, or you can go horseback riding, ballooning, or golf—all nearby. At the end of the week there is a farewell dinner at a well-known restaurant where participants receive a diploma, an apron, and a Jane Butel cookbook.

MEALS AND ACCOMMODATIONS—Daily continental breakfast, five lavish lunches, and two dinners at noted restaurants are included. You stay in deluxe rooms in the La Posada Hotel, the only historic-landmark hotel in Albuquerque (one of 210 in the United States), which also houses the cooking school.

FELLOW PARTICIPANTS—No more than eighteen people in a class. Ages range from an occasional teen to seniors, about half men and half women, married and single people.

PRICE—$1,995 for double occupancy; single supplement, $350. Airfare is not included.

Smithsonian Study Tours
2 Berkeley St.
Boston, MA 02116
(877) 338-8687
www.smithsonianstudytours.org

Each year the Smithsonian offers over 350 study tours and seminars all over the world. This is the nation's largest museum-based educational travel program. Tour concepts and destinations reflect the diverse interests of the Smithsonian. They include cultural tours, study voyages on the great rivers and waterways of the world, countryside tours with lectures and activities in a town or region, tours of the grand cities of the world and their outstanding cultural offerings, natural history tours that provide active journeys through the scenic and natural wonders of the world, and weekend trips to see the treasures of the Smithsonian Institute in Washington, D.C.

WHERE—Worldwide.

PRICE—$1,000 to $10,000 for double occupancy; single supplement is very variable. Airfare is included with some trips.

Ancient Capitals of Beijing and Xi'an, with an optional extension to Shanghai (twelve days)

Participants will explore these historic capitals and their timeless treasures. You learn about the history of these ancient places through lectures given by your study leader and guided excursions to major sites and museums. The journey includes a visit to a kindergarten and a private home to meet the friendly people of modern China and discover how they preserve their heritage today.

In Beijing you visit such famous sites as the Forbidden City, the Temple of Heaven, Tiananmen Square (often the scene of mass meetings, parades, celebrations, and demonstrations), Ming tombs, and the Great Wall of China. In Xi'an you have the opportunity to attend demonstrations that reflect Chinese culture, such as meeting a well-known artist during a calligraphy lesson and observing the traditional culinary skills of noodle-making. Excursions and lectures introduce you to the area's most treasured sites including the Museum of the Stone Stele, the Banpo Neolithic Museum (a covered excavation of a 6,000-year-old village) and the Terra-Cotta Warriors, the famous buried army of terra-cotta warriors, part of the burial of the first Qin emperor, who reigned from 221 to 209 B.C. In all, there are more than 7,000 individually crafted life-size soldiers and horses that were meant to protect the emperor after his death. If you wish to experience the modern vitality of the great port of Shanghai, this tour extension leaves from Xi'an on the tenth day of the journey.

MEALS AND ACCOMMODATIONS—With the extension, eleven breakfasts, ten lunches, and six dinners are included. In Beijing you stay at the Beijing International, a first-class hotel located in the heart of the city. You stay at the Grand New World Hotel in Xi'an located in the center of Xi'an, within the old city walls.

FELLOW TRAVELERS—Well-educated, curious people take this tour, an equal number of men and women of all ages, singles and couples.

PRICE—$2,899 to $3,899 for double occupancy; single supplement, $239. Optional excursion to Shanghai, $579 for single occupancy. Airfare is included.

John C. Campbell Folk School
One Folk Road
Brasstown, NC 28902
(800) FOLK-SCH (365-5724)
www.folkschool.org

This school offers instructive one-week classes and weekend classes in a wide variety of crafts rooted in the traditions of southern Appalachia and other cultures around the world. These include everything from basketry, crocheting, drawing, embroidery, enameling, painting, paper art, quilting, spinning, wood carving, weaving, and woodworking among others. There are also classes in photography, writing, story telling and nature studies. Nestled between the Great Smoky Mountains and the Blue Ridge, the school is set on 380 acres and was founded in 1925.

MEALS AND ACCOMMODATIONS—Three family-style meals are served daily in the dining hall, featuring the regional cooking of southern Appalachia. Students with special dietary needs and vegetarians are accommodated. Lodgings are dorm rooms with several twin beds and a shared bath, rooms with two twin beds and a bath accessible from the hallway, and rooms with two twin beds and a bath in the room. Room assignments are made at the discretion of the registrar according to the space available.

SAMPLE WEEK—Your stay begins on Sunday. Registration is from 3:00 to 5:30 P.M. Dinner is at 6:00 P.M. Monday morning begins with a refreshing group walk through the woods at 7:15 A.M. MorningSong begins at 7:45 A.M. This Danish custom of singing, folklore, and camaraderie is led by someone different each week. After breakfast, everyone moves across campus to the classrooms, located in the many studios at the Folk School. Morning classes last from 9:00 A.M. until noon. Classes resume at 1:30 P.M. and last until 4:30 P.M. In your free time you can visit a local pottery studio, a blacksmith's shop, or the local artists' shops, or you can browse through the Folk School's craft shop. After-dinner activities include folk music, folklore, and stories or a slide presentation. The week ends on Friday with the student exhibit, where you can display the results of your work and view the creations of your new friends. That night there is a concert with bluegrass, old-time, and other types of music born in this area. You leave on Saturday.

FELLOW PARTICIPANTS—Most classes are limited to twelve students; there are people of all ages, both men and women.

PRICE—Each class costs $268 for a week. Weekend classes are $168. Accommodations and meals cost $223 to $300. Airfare is not included.

British Network Ltd.
112 W. High St.
Carlisle, PA 17013
(800) 274-8583
www.britishnetworkltd.com

This tour operator takes pride in offering "behind the tourist facade" tours. Its more than 250 trips include a wide variety of themes such as homes and gardens, literature, and battles in northern France. The tours are designed to be flexible in order to take advantage of special sights and events. You definitely see the well-known sights, but from a different angle. The company's goal is to show you the *real* country, where people live, not just the monuments and museums.All tours are leisurely paced.

WHERE—England, Scotland, Wales, Ireland, France, Poland, Italy, Belgium, and Holland.

PRICE—$599 to $2,529 for double occupancy; single supplement, $135 to $595. Airfare is not included.

London and England's Castles and Gardens (nine days)

This tour is an exploration of London and the English countryside that shows the best of the city, castles, and historic gardens. The tour begins in London, where you visit the royal family's castles and historic gardens. Next, you head out of London via motor coach to enjoy a private visit to Leeds Castle, often called the loveliest castle in the world, set in the middle of a lake and surrounded by beautifully manicured lawns. Then it's on to Canterbury and its cathedral. The trip continues to the White Cliffs of Dover, renowned for its castle and great stretch of white chalk cliffs. Other highlights include the Ham House, an outstanding 1610 Stuart house on the banks of the Thames River that contains rare surviving furnishings of the seventeenth century. You then go to Kent, the "Garden of England," where you visit some of the loveliest gardens in the area. Another garden visit is Sissinghurst Castle Garden, made up of small, enclosed romantic gardens each with its own color scheme.

MEALS AND ACCOMMODATIONS—All breakfasts and dinners. You stay at a centrally located hotel reflecting English charm.

FELLOW TRAVELERS—The group consists of a maximum of sixteen people from all walks of life.

PRICE—$2,250 for double occupancy; single supplement, $560. Airfare is not included.

Hibiscus Tours
885 Third Ave., Suite 2900
New York, NY 10022
(800) 653-0802
www.hibiscustours.com

This company offers cultural tours. The operators will also customize a tour for you. Their special interest tours include: Food and Wine in Eastern Europe; Culinary Adventures along the Silk Road; Art along the Silk Road; Islamic Art and Architecture; Architecture of North Africa; Hidden Treasures of Eastern Europe; Hong Kong in a New Light; Jewish heritage tours; Christian tours; professional medical and legal tours; horticulture tours, and much more. Hibiscus also handles unusual spa destinations.

WHERE—Asia, Central Asia, Near East, Africa, Eastern Europe, Canada.

PRICE—$150 to $500 a day for single accommodations.

Pushkin Literary Tour (ten days)

You arrive in St. Petersburg, Russia. Sight-seeing highlights include a city tour, Nabokov's museum flat, the Kazan Cathedral and a visit to the Pushkin Museum Flat. You lunch at the Literaturnoye Café, which is housed where Pushkin met his "aide" before going to his duel. Other interesting stops include the world-famous Hermitage Museum and Dostoyevsky's museum flat and the locations of his duel. You also see the town of Pushkin, where you visit the Pushkin Dacha where Pushkin and his wife had their honeymoon in 1831, and much more. A five-hour ride through picturesque Russian countryside takes you to Pskov. Other highlights are Pushkinskiye Gory, where you visit the Pushkin family burial place and a former Pushkin family estate that is now a museum. Returning to St. Petersburg, you have time for optional tours and shopping on your own.

MEALS AND ACCOMMODATIONS—Included are eight breakfasts, seven lunches, and three dinners. You have your choice of five-star, four-star, or three-star hotels.

FELLOW TRAVELERS—Participants are usually affluent, well-educated men and women, ages from thirty-five to seventy-five. They are well traveled and interested in visiting different destinations in the arts, music, literature, food, and architecture of different cultures.

PRICE—$3,599 for double occupancy in a five-star hotel; single supplement, $699; $3,299 double occupancy in a four-star hotel; single supplement, $449; $2,549 for double occupancy in a three-star hotel; single supplement, $299. Airfare is not included.

Educational Travel Services
5725 Imperial Lakes Blvd.
Mulberry, FL 33860
(800) 929-4387
www.travelwithus.com

This company is the largest tour operator in the United States specializing in Christian pilgrimages to the Holy Land.

WHERE—Worldwide.

PRICE—$1,700 to $2,500 for double occupancy; single supplement, $320 to $398. Airfare is included.

Italy 2001 (ten days)

Your Italian adventure begins in Milan where your sight-seeing tour includes the white marble Duomo Cathedral and the Teatro alla Scalla, the most famous opera house in the world. You also visit Verona, immortalized in Shakespeare's *Romeo and Juliet*. Then it's on to the city in the sea, Venice. Here you visit St. Mark's, one of the world's most magnificent churches, and other important sites. The tour continues to Florence with much sight-seeing, including the Santa Maria del Fiore Cathedral, which houses Michelangelo's unfinished Pieta, and the Baptistry, which features Ghiberti's famous Gates of Paradise. The tour continues to Assissi, the medieval town that was home to St. Francis. Your next city is Rome, the Eternal City. Here you visit the Vatican and the Sistine Chapel. You also tour ancient Rome with its many attractions such as the Spanish Steps and Trevi Fountain. Legend has it that those who toss a coin into the fountain will one day return to Rome to toss another into the waters of Trevi. From here it is *arrivederci* to Italy.

MEALS AND ACCOMMODATIONS—Continental breakfast and a set-menu dinner daily are included. You stay in superior tourist or first-class hotels.

FELLOW TRAVELERS—Christians of all ages, usually women.

PRICE—$1,998 to $2,298 for double occupancy; single supplement, $395. Airfare is included.

Catholic Travel Office
10018 Cedar Lane
Kensington, MD 20895
(301) 530-8963
www.catholictraveloffice.com

This organization's pilgrimages are designed to visit sacred places on special dates, such as the Holy Land at Christmas time.

WHERE—Israel, Europe, and China.

PRICE—$1,250 to $2,700 for double occupancy; single supplement, $30 a day.

Christmas Holy Land Pilgrimage (fifteen days)

This fifteen-day tour takes you to Israel with visits to Jerusalem, Bethlehem, Nazareth, Tiberias, and Tel Aviv, and then to Rome, Italy. Tour highlights include numerous important religious sites.

MEALS AND ACCOMMODATIONS—All meals are included in Israel, but only breakfast is included in Rome. Hotels are standard class.

FELLOW TRAVELERS—Single women, traveling alone or with a friend, make up 40 to 50 percent of the participants.

PRICE—$2,275 for double occupancy; single supplement, $30 a day. Airfare from New York is included.

Ayelet Tours
24 Wade Rd.
Latham, NY 12110
(800) 237-1517
www.ayelet.com

This company offers fully escorted Christian and Jewish heritage tours.

WHERE—Israel, Egypt, Morocco, Turkey, Eastern Europe, China, South America, Italy, Germany.

PRICE—$1,499 to $4,000 for double occupancy; single supplement is very variable. Airfare is not included.

Eastern Europe (thirteen days)

This trip includes visits to cities in Poland, Hungary, and the Czech Republic. The tour begins with your arrival in Warsaw and a two-night stay there. Among the places you visit are the Warsaw Ghetto, Nozyk Synagogue, and the Old Jewish Cemetery. Next you go to Krakow for two nights, where you visit the Jewish district of Kazimierz, Oskar Schindler's factory, the Plashow concentration camp, and much more. The following day you see Auschwitz. You then continue on to Budapest for a four-night stay. Here you visit the Dohany Synagogue, the Jewish Cemetery, the Jewish Museum, and much more. A short flight then takes you to Prague for a three-night stay. The numerous points of interest you visit include Wallenstein Garden, Alt-New Synagogue, the Astronomical Clock, and St. Vitus Cathedral.

MEALS AND ACCOMMODATIONS—The price includes all breakfasts and four dinners. The hotels are four-star, all with full-service restaurants.

FELLOW TRAVELERS—Men and women, couples and singles, usually from the age of forty and up.

PRICE—$2,899 for double occupancy; single supplement, $549. Airfare from New York City is included. The tour does not include the flight from Budapest to Prague (approximate cost, $150).

St. John's Abbey
St. John's University
Collegeville, MN 56321
(320) 363-2573

Some visitors come to St. John's to have a spiritual retreat for a weekend or several days. Others come just to relax and "get away from it all," or to talk to the monks about their spiritual life. Still others come to experience the architecture of the buildings. All guests are invited to pray with the monks and to enjoy the beauty and serenity of the 2,480 acres of prairie, wetlands, forests, and lakes.

MEALS AND ACCOMMODATIONS—Meals are available in the Abbey's guest dining room. The cost per day is $3.50 for continental breakfast, $5.75 for lunch, and $6.75 for dinner. There are a limited number of guest rooms (all with private baths) at the Abbey.

PRICE—Spiritual direction sessions are $30 each, or whatever you are able to offer. Overnight accommodations in the abbey are $26 for a single room and $35 for a double occupancy.

American Jewish Congress Worldwide Tours
15 East 84th St.
New York, NY 10028
(800) 221-4694
www.ajcongresstravel.com

The goal of this Jewish organization's tour program is to give you a glimpse of Jewish life around the world, but it also includes the sites no American would dream of missing. Some of its tours are specifically geared to singles aged twenty-nine to forty-nine.

WHERE—Israel, India, Turkey, Morocco, Spain, France, England, Ireland, Italy, Poland, the Netherlands.

PRICE—$2,800 to $5,000 for double occupancy; single supplements are very variable up to $500. Airfare from New York City is included.

The Grand Tour of Spain for Singles—Ages Twenty-Nine to Forty-Nine (fifteen days including Gibraltar)

A milennium ago, Spain was the center of the Jewish world. The tour begins in Madrid and continues to Toledo, once the royal capital of Spain and the heart of Jewish learning and literature. After returning to Madrid for more sight-seeing you visit the plains of La Mancha, made famous by Cervantes. Then it's on to the Andalusian city of Granada, and then Alhambra, where in 1492 Ferdinand and Isabella signed the decree expelling all Jews from

Spain. Cordoba is next with a visit to the pre-Inquisition Jewish Quarter. Other stops include Seville and the elegant resort town of Marbella. On the way you see the Rock of Gibraltar's legendary Barbary apes and the ancient Jewish cemetery (Jews have lived in Gibraltar for at least five hundred years). A flight from Marbella takes you to the magnificent city of Barcelona, home of the 1992 Olympic Games, for a four-night stay and visits to numerous locations of Jewish significance. After a day of leisure you return home.

MEALS AND ACCOMMODATIONS—Included are all breakfasts, one lunch, and nine dinners, plus unscheduled treats and in-flight meals. The hotels are first class and deluxe.

FELLOW TRAVELERS—Jewish Americans from all fifty states; ages twenty-nine to forty-nine.

PRICE—$3,795 to $3,895 for double occupancy; single supplement, $625. Airfare from New York City is included.

Blue Voyage Tours and Travel LLC
323 Geary St., Suite 401
San Francisco, CA 94102
(800) 81-TURKEY

As part of their broad range of tours in Turkey and Greece, this company offers a ten-day Jewish tour in Turkey. The tour begins in Istanbul. Sight-seeing begins with a visit to Galata, a Jewish neighborhood and site of the Galata Tower, built by the Genoese in 1303. You visit the Ashkenazi Synagogue and the Shalom Synagogue, the biggest one in Istanbul. Other stops include the Blue Mosque, the St. Sophia Church, and the Balat district. Dating back to 1492, the Balat district is the oldest Jewish neighborhood in Istanbul, and the Star of David is found on the facades of many of the buildings in the area. The next stops are the Ahrida Synagogue and the Yanbol Synagogue, which date back to the Byzantine period, and more. A short airplane ride takes you to Izmir—on the Aegean Sea—whose Jewish community is around 2,000 years old.

Then you drive to the Ionian cities Miletus and Priene. Other visits include Sardis and its synagogues that date back to the third century B.C. You then return to Istanbul and spend the remaining time at your leisure exploring this wonderful city.

MEALS AND ACCOMMODATIONS—Included are eight breakfasts, five lunches, and six dinners. You have a choice of first class or deluxe hotels.

FELLOW TRAVELERS—Jewish singles and couples, all ages.

PRICE—$1,495 for double occupancy in a first-class hotel; $240, single supplement; $1,699 for double occupancy in a deluxe hotel; single supplement, $365. Airfare is not included.

11

Spa Vacations

Our life is frittered away by detail . . . Simplify, simplify.—Henry David Thoreau

A spa vacation is the best present you can give yourself. Imagine escaping to a serene oasis where both your body and mind are attended to with the utmost care and comfort. You're energized by state-of-the-art fitness facilities, toned, destressed, and treated with the very latest in pampering paraphernalia.

For the solo traveler, spas offer instant camaraderie as many women choose to go it alone. Another plus is that going about your activities in comfortable attire, shorts, polos, or sweats all day makes it very easy to get to know others; it's a great "leveler." If you choose a resort spa there is usually a hospitality desk where they pair single people together in the dining room. Or, if you wish, you can remain totally alone. Many resort spas have room service for total relaxation.

All spas offer a variety of activities throughout the day; there's something for everyone. You can be as active and athletic as you wish, or just relax and let yourself be coddled from head to toe with an assortment of massage and beauty treatments. For the health conscious, there are spas that offer a medical consultation, low-fat cooking demonstrations, nutrition and alternative medicine classes, in addition to catering to your beauty needs from head to toe. If you want to burn off extra pounds or are seeking expert destressing techniques, and wish to feel the tension escaping from every pore in your body, there's a special spa to suit your needs.

Hunger is not allowed at spas. Yes, some are dedicated to weight management and healthful diet, but the one thing they all have in common is they make sure no one ever leaves the table hungry. Expert chefs create meals that are well-balanced, nutritious, and delicious. You get to enjoy your dining experience yet still lose pounds and inches thanks to the low fat content of the food.

As with any vacation, you must decide what is most important to you. Do you want to go to a spa where the main focus is on beauty and the pleasures of being pampered or to one more dedicated to health issues, such as lowering cholesterol and improving tranquility? Do you want to go to a spa that is attached to a resort or hotel offering vacation options like golf? If you decide on a resort spa, and are looking for total relaxation, you may not wish to go when children are out of school and likely to accompany their parents.

Another choice is between a coed spa or a ladies-only facility. Do you want a small spa or a large one? What kind of climate and atmosphere do you prefer: secluded in the mountains, close to a city, or by the ocean? There are spas all over the United States as well as abroad. Spas also vary considerably in price, from inexpensive to luxurious high-priced.

Many spas will transfer you to and from an airport or train station. Everything is arranged for you.

Here are some tips to help you enjoy your spa vacation to the fullest:

- Leave your business matters and problems home. Don't think of the spa as a place for "catching up." Tell your work and family not to call.
- Bring comfortable attire. Check with the spa to see what they recommend. If you're going to do a lot of walking or hiking,

make sure you have the right kind of sneakers. Wear them before you arrive so you know they're comfortable. Bring a waistband with an attachment for a water bottle (you need to drink plenty of water throughout the day's activities). If you're going to a hot climate, bring plenty of sunscreen and a hat.

- Try something new. Just because you've never done it before doesn't mean you shouldn't ever do it. Spas have all kinds of beauty aids as well as classes and machines that may be new to you but that can be very beneficial. You don't know until you try.
- Ask for the staff's help. That's what they're there for. Ask questions. Let them help you with the machines, etc.
- Be friendly to everyone. Sit with different people at each meal for the first couple of days. Talk with a variety of people in class and on walks or hikes. The bonds you make can be lasting.
- Listen to your body, and heed what it tells you. Only you know when you've done enough exercise or need a rest, regardless of what others are doing. Every individual in a class is at a different level of fitness. Do not hesitate to slow down when you feel you should, but do it gradually. Reducing your activity level while continuing to keep up some movement is preferable to suddenly stopping all activity.
- Learn to deep-breathe. Periodically take a long breath and let it out. This will enhance your energy and relaxation.

A good way to locate a spa to suit your individual needs is to call SPA-FINDERS, a well-known spa and resort travel company, at (800) ALL-SPAS (255-7727) or (212) 924-7173. Its Web site address is www.spafinder.com.

Here are various types of spas in many different destinations. You can call them or SPA-FINDERS to make a reservation or to get more information.

Golden Door

PO Box 463077
Escondido, CA 92046
(800) 424-0777
www.goldendoor.com

With its formal Japanese gardens, this luxurious spa replicates a Japanese honjin inn. Occupancy is limited to thirty-nine guests cared for by a staff of 160. The food is celebrated haute spa cuisine made with produce picked daily in Golden Door's own organic orchards.

FACILITIES—Aerobics, yoga, meditation, Tai Chi, hiking, tennis, weight and cardiovascular equipment, indoor and outdoor pools, massage, and body, skin care, and beauty treatments. In addition, before-bed minimassages are given in your own room.

PRICE—$5,725 for seven nights. This includes single accommodations, three meals daily, full exercise programs, beauty hour, herbal wraps, aqua aerobics, yoga, massages, a hot tub, and evening programs.

Cal-a-Vie

2249 Somerset Road
Vista, CA 92084
(866) 772-4283
www.cal-a-vie.com

This elegant 150-acre spa resembles a small village in Provence. Guests reside in twenty-four private cottages decorated with flowered chintzes and carved wood furnishings, and dine on gourmet cuisine.

FACILITIES—Aerobics, yoga, hiking, golf, tennis, weight and cardiovascular equipment, an outdoor pool, body treatments, massage, skin care treatments, a beauty salon, hydrotherapy.

PRICE—$5,150 for a seven-night stay. The price includes single accommodations, three spa meals daily, sixteen spa treatments, full fitness programs, and evening programs.

Miraval, Life in Balance
5000 East Via Estancia Miraval
Catalina, AZ 85739
(800) 825-4000
www.miravalresort.com

Located on thirty acres of scenic Arizona desert, Miraval has a Zen garden desert, a botanical garden, and a four-hundred-seat auditorium. Their emphasis is more on stress-reduction, self-discovery, and mind-body interaction than on diet, fitness, and traditional therapies. Yet nothing is spared in the pampering and luxury department.

FACILITIES—Aerobics, yoga, and meditation, hiking, golf, tennis, horseback riding, bicycling, weight and cardiovascular equipment, fitness profiles, three swimming pools, body and skin care treatments, a beauty salon. They also offer spectacular rock climbing, a challenging athletic program called Quantum Leap, and other specially designed activities.

PRICE—$840 to $2,625 for three to seven nights depending on the time of year. The price includes single accommodations, three meals daily, and unlimited use of resort facilities. It also includes one personal service per night such as massage, pedicure, or facial.

The Broadmoor
PO Box 1439
Colorado Springs, CO 80901
(800) 634-7711

The Broadmoor, the most distinguished of the Colorado Rockies resorts, recently opened a world-class spa. The hotel itself is regularly a proud winner of the coveted Mobil Five Star and AAA

Five Diamond awards. It has nine restaurants, including one with Edwardian decor that serves continental cuisine, a '50s-style sidewalk café, and a restaurant that features healthful cuisine served in the Golf Club dining room.

FACILITIES—Aerobics, Cybex weight resistance and cardiovascular equipment; sixteen massage rooms; wet treatment rooms for wraps, hydrotherapy, aromatherapy, and Vichy showers; meditation; a beauty salon; an indoor pool. For outdoor activity there are fifty-four holes of championship golf, twelve all-weather tennis courts, horseback riding, hiking, and cross-country skiing.

PRICE—$1,122 to $1,569 for three nights. The price includes single accommodations, a daily spa package consisting of your choice of skin and body treatments, use of the facilities, and more.

Chateau Elan
Haven Harbour Dr.
Braselton, GA 30517
(800) 233-9463

Chateau Elan started as a vineyard in the rich soil of Georgia not far from Atlanta. Now guests come here to see the sixteenth-century French-style chateau and to enjoy excellent food and wine and the intimate, European-style health spa. The Chateau offers both casual fare in an open-air setting and dining with fine china and Irish crystal, for those who prefer a more formal style.

FACILITIES—Aerobics, yoga, hiking, golf, bicycling, body treatment, massage, skin care treatments, beauty salon.

PRICE—$889 to $2,299 for two to five nights. The price includes single accommodations; three meals daily; a variety of skin and body treatments, according to the package; steambaths; a sauna; a whirlpool; an indoor resistance pool; a fitness area and classes; afternoon tea; a complimentary winery tour with tastings.

The Inn at Manitou
77 Ingram Dr. Suite 200
Toronto, ON M6M 207
Canada
(011) 44-128-357-5671 or 800-571-8818

This is one of the worlds premier luxury tennis resorts with a spa, set on a 550-acre private forest. The inn's acclaimed kitchen boasts twelve French chefs and offers a specially created spa menu of 1,400 to 1,600 calories daily.

FACILITIES—The inn has thirteen tennis courts, twelve teaching professionals, and an exciting program of clinics and instruction tailored to the needs of players at all levels. Also offered are aerobics, hiking, golf, horseback riding, bicycling, boating, weight and cardiovascular equipment, fitness profiles, an outdoor pool, body and skin care treatments, a beauty salon, and hydrotherapy.

PRICE—$998 to $2,383 for three to seven nights. The price includes single accommodations; a fruit basket; three meals daily; tea and scones daily; fruit, herbal tea, and juice breaks; choices of skin and body treatments, according to the package; tennis courts, mountain bikes, sailboats, canoes, and exercise equipment; and a consultation with the spa director.

The Regency House
2000 South Ocean Drive
Hallandale, FL 33009
(800) 454-0003
www.regencyhealthspa.com

Located on a white, sandy beach in southern Florida, the Regency House is dedicated to the concept of holistic living. Many guests lose up to ten pounds a week. Vegetarian meals are served.

FACILITIES—Aerobics, yoga and meditation, boating, weight and cardiovascular equipment, fitness profiles, an outdoor pool, body treatments, massage, skin care treatments, a beauty salon.

PRICE—$1,095 to $1,395 (according to the season) for seven nights. The price includes single accommodations, three vegetarian meals daily, medically supervised juice or water fasting, two spa services per week; health consultations; cooking demonstrations; supervised exercise programs; and full use of the facilities.

Vatra Mountain Valley Health Resort
PO Box F
Hunter, NY 12442
(800) 232-2772

This lovely resort, tucked away in the beautiful Catskill Mountains, offers an active weight-loss and fitness program. Healthful low-calorie vegetarian meals that won't leave you hungry are served in the cozy, country dining room. Pampering massage treatments are included in the various packages, and a wide choice of other skin-care and body treatments are available.

FACILITIES—Aerobics, meditation, hiking, golf, tennis, horseback riding, weight and cardiovascular equipment, fitness profiles, indoor and outdoor pools, body and skin care treatments, a beauty salon, hydrotherapy.

PRICE—$525 to $1,295 for three-night to seven-night packages. The price includes single accommodations, three vegetarian meals daily, spa treatments according to the package, participation in full-day fitness programs, exercise classes, use of the facilities, and evening entertainment.

The Spa at Grand Lake
1667 Exeter Rd.
Lebanon, CT 06249
(800) 843-7721

The atmosphere at this spa is casual and friendly. Rooms are comfortably furnished with private baths, television, and air-conditioning. Evening activities typically include live music, a video, or a lecture. A nurse is available twenty-four hours a day to answer your questions and help you plan an effective weight loss and fitness program.

FACILITIES—Aerobics, yoga, golf, hiking, tennis, weight and cardiovascular equipment, indoor and outdoor pools, body treatment and massage, skin care treatments, a beauty salon.

PRICE—$400 for two-night packages; $639 to $719 for four-night packages; $999 to $1,099 for seven-night packages. The price includes single accommodations, three meals daily, one half-hour massage for each night of your stay, exercise classes, nutritional seminars, and use of the spa facilities.

Rancho La Puerta
PO Box 69
Tecate, CA 91980
(800) 443-7565

This ranch occupies 3,000 acres of lush oasis surrounded by unspoiled countryside. Each cottage has its own patio garden and is decorated with colorful Mexican folk art. The cuisine features freshly picked produce grown in Rancho's own six-acre organic garden.

FACILITIES—Aerobics, yoga and meditation, hiking, tennis, weight and cardiovascular equipment, fitness profiles, an outdoor pool, body treatments, massage, a beauty salon, mind/body/spirit classes in yoga, Tai Chi, meditation.

PRICE—$1,745 to $1,985 for seven-night programs. The price includes single accommodations, three spa cuisine meals daily; use of facilities, tennis courts, gyms, swimming pools, and hiking trails; exercise classes; evening program; and films. Summer rates also include one massage and one herbal wrap.

Red Mountain Spa
22 N. Snow Canyon Road
Ivins, UT 84738
(800) 407-3002

Set in the best scenery Mother Nature has to offer in southwestern Utah's red sandstone country at the mouth of Snow Canyon, and offering the utmost in healthy living, this spa is too good to keep under wraps. In fact, *Shape* magazine has called Red Mountain "the best outdoor fitness program located in the most scenic area of any spa."

Red Mountain has a desert climate that makes it perfect for year-round outdoor activities. The spa's main emphasis is on changing peoples lifestyles, and it succeeds. Its excellent fitness and weight-loss program, as well as its health-promoting programs, makes this one of our favorite spas. Many guests actually lower their cholesterol levels and lose significant weight during their stay. Guests can enjoy either vegetarian meals or a modified diet that includes small amounts of poultry and fish. Each day there are lectures on nutrition, exercise, the spa's philosophy of living, and cooking classes taught by the executive chef. And there's still plenty of time to keep up with the excellent beauty treatments. The greatest benefits of Red Mountain are best recognized when you get home with a feeling of renewal and a commitment to a healthier lifestyle.

FACILITIES—Aerobics, yoga, hiking, tennis, spinning, horseback riding, bicycling, weight and cardiovascular equipment, fitness profiles, indoor pools, massage, skin care treatments, a beauty salon.

PRICE—$1,399 to $4,476 for six nights to twenty-seven nights. The price includes single accommodations, three low-fat meals daily, lectures, exercise programs, personal fitness evaluations, cardio-vascular endurance tests.

Deerfield Manor Spa
650 Resica Falls Rd.
E. Stroudsberg, PA 18301
(800) 852-4494

This charming country spa is located in the Pocono Mountains of Pennsylvania, an easy drive from New York City, Philadelphia, or Washington, D.C. Delicious low-calorie meals are served in the cozy dining room, where fresh flowers and fine linens add elegance to every meal. Guest rooms are decorated in the Laura Ashley style. Fascinating lectures and entertainment are featured every day.

FACILITIES—Aerobics, yoga, Tai Chi, hiking, tennis, horseback riding nearby, weight and cardiovascular equipment, fitness profiles, an outdoor pool, body treatments, massage, skin care treatments.

PRICE—$404 to $1,024 for two-night to seven-night packages. The price includes single accommodations; three meals daily; fitness programs including aerobics, flexibility, toning, and more; use of the facilities; evening entertainment.

New Age Health Spa
Rt. 55
Neversink, NY 12765
(914) 985-7601 or (800) 682-4348
www.newagehealthspa.com

This spa is located on 160 acres of rolling hills in the Catskill Mountains just two hours' drive from New York City. The focus is on both a wide array of fitness activities and its holistic philosophy. The spa offers special meal plans for weight loss or weight control. Many of the vegetables and herbs are organically grown in the spa's own greenhouse. Rustic accommodations offer beautiful views of the woods, hills, and mountains.

FACILITIES—Aerobics, yoga, hiking, tennis, horseback riding, cross-country skiing, weight and cardiovascular equipment, fitness profiles, indoor and outdoor pools, body treatments, massage, skin care treatments, a beauty salon.

PRICE—$193 to $233 nightly; $965 to $1,364 for five to seven nights. The price includes single accommodations, three meals daily (a juice fasting diet is available), use of the spa facilities, a complete fitness day, evening programs, and outdoor activities.

Gurney's Inn Resort & Spa
290 Old Montauk Highway
Montauk, NY 11954
(631) 668-2345
www.gurneys-inn.com

This spa is located on the east end of Long Island along one of the world's most beautiful private beaches. It has been rated one of "best in the world" by *Vogue* magazine. Meals are served in the resort's dining room, which affords a spectacular view of the ocean. The food is low in salt, saturated fat, cholesterol, and refined carbohydrates, but full of variety and flavor, featuring fresh foods according to season.

FACILITIES—Aerobics; yoga; hiking; golf; horseback riding; bicycling; boating; water sports; weight and cardiovascular equipment; fitness profiles; an indoor seawater pool; seawater Roman baths; Swiss showers; aquatic exercise classes; more than thirty-five massage, beauty, and body therapies including acupuncture, samadhi (combining acupuncture, cranio-sacral therapy, and acupressure), reiki, and green active argelite mud therapy; a beauty salon.

PRICE—$200 to $300 nightly. The price includes single accommodations, three meals daily, use of the spa facilities, a morning beach walk, lectures, and unlimited classes. Spa services are available a la carte.

Ixtapa Hotel & Spa
Tonala 177 Esquina Yactan Cobniarona
06700 Mexico, DF Mexico
(011) 52-714-3-00-73

Located where the ancient Aztec emperor Montezuma used to come to enjoy the therapeutic mineral springs, this resort recently underwent extensive renovations. It updated its fitness center and created a beautiful new spa treatment center. A variety of packages are available, including the Diet Package for guests who want to lose weight, improve fitness, and receive beauty treatments. The Relax Package is for people who need to destress, with yoga classes, shiatsu massage, and acupuncture sessions. For those who want to challenge their fitness level there is the Sports Package, which offers mountain bike rides and excursions to interesting sites in the surrounding area balanced with sport intensive massages. The special four-week Vibrance Package allows guests to experience all of the above plus Spanish lessons.

FACILITIES—Aerobics, yoga, hiking, golf, tennis, boating, weight and cardiovascular equipment, fitness profiles, an outdoor pool, massage, body and skin care treatments, a beauty salon, hydrotherapy.

PRICE—$520 to $4,500 for four-night to twenty-eight-night packages. The price includes single accommodations, three meals daily, daily skin and body treatments according to the package (a week's stay includes a daily massage and facial and numerous other treatments), morning walks, aerobic and exercise sessions, yoga, golf or tennis lessons, and use of the facilities.

Fiesta Americana Condesa
Blvd. Kukulcan Kn.16.5
Zona Hotelera 7500
Cancun, QR Mexico
(011) 52-988-5-10-00

This impressive resort enjoys a lush setting amid tropical foliage, cascading waterfalls, and the clear turquoise waters of the Caribbean right outside. Accommodations are luxurious as well, boasting oak furniture, marble baths, and private balconies. Rooms are equipped with purified water systems, climate control, satellite TV, and direct-dial telephones. Restaurants feature northern Italian, seafood, gourmet international, Mexican, and Caribbean.

FACILITIES—Aerobics, golf, tennis, horseback riding, boating, water sports, weight and cardiovascular equipment, fitness profiles, an outdoor pool, a beauty salon. Over forty body, skin, and hair treatments are offered.

PRICE—$751 to $1,123 for a three-night package. The price includes single accommodations, a daily buffet breakfast, your choice of daily lunch or dinner, three treatments with a choice of facial, body therapy, or antistress massage, one hour of indoor tennis per day.

Spas Abroad
Hyatt Regency Hotel Dead Seas
Ei'n Bokek
Dead Sea 86908, Israel
(011) 972-3-624-1345

Spa lovers from all over the world come to the Dead Sea because of its intensely rich minerals and for the mud that's found in this region. And because the Dead Sea is the lowest point on earth, the area is thought to be the safest place to sunbathe.

This hotel features six hundred luxurious rooms, each with a private balcony overlooking the Dead Sea. There are three restaurants in the hotel (kosher food is available), a bar, and a nightclub, as well as a camp for children.

FACILITIES—Tennis, weight and cardiovascular equipment, massage rooms, mud bath rooms, a dry sauna, steam rooms, a sulphur bath, a Dead Sea–water pool, skin care treatments, a beauty salon, hydrotherapy.

PRICE—$1,572 to $2,394 for four- to seven-night packages. The price includes single accommodations, breakfast and dinner daily, daily treatments including skin consultations, facials, massage, and more; use of the spa and the fitness facilities, including exercise classes, squash, and tennis.

Moriah Plaza Dead Sea Spa
Sheraton Moriah Plaza Dead Sea Hotel
Sodom 84960, Israel
(011) 972-7-659-7591

This family-style hotel with its own in-house spa is located on a private beach. The spa specializes in Dead Sea–water hydrotherapy, offering a choice of treatment programs.

FACILITIES—Tennis, weight and cardiovascular equipment, an indoor heated Dead Sea–water pool and a freshwater outdoor pool, basketball, jogging, dry massage, underwater massage, inhalation treatment, beauty salon, hydrotheraphy.

PRICE—$1,740 to $1,905 for a seven-night beauty package; $1,640 to $1,795 for a seven-night rheumatic package. The price includes single accommodations, two meals daily, skin and body treatments according to the package, exercise classes, use of the facilities, tennis courts, a fitness center, indoor and outdoor pools, direct access to the beach, and evening entertainment.

Margitsziget Island
H-1138 Budapest
Margitsziget, Hungary
Budapest, Hungary
(011) 36-1-452-6277

Because Hungary is rich in medicinal thermal springs, spas have long been part of its culture. Budapest has historically been famous for its baths, and people still come here for that purpose. The most elegant baths are located on Margitsziget Island, which is wedged between Buda and Pest in the Danube River. The thermal waters here were first brought to the surface in 1866. The Thermal Hotel Margitsziget was completed in 1979 as the world's first metropolitan health resort hotel, just ten minutes by car from downtown Budapest. Connected by tunnel and sharing the modern spa facilities is the palatial Grand Hotel Margitsziget. Built 118 years ago, it has recently been restored to its original splendor.

FACILITIES—Horseback riding, bicycling, an indoor pool, body treatments, skin care treatments, a beauty salon, hydrotherapy. The spa equipment features the most modern thermal bath and physiotherapy equipment, including thermal pools, a sauna, underwater jet massage, a carbon gas bath, therapeutic gymnastics, massage, mud packs, and a solarium.

PRICE—$658 to $1,224 for seven nights to twenty-one nights. The price includes single accommodations, two meals daily, one welcome cocktail, a medical examination, spa and thermal treatments as prescribed by a physician, use of the facilities.

Hoar Cross Hall Health Resort
Hoar Cross Hall, Hoar Cross
Near Yoxall
Staffordshire, DE13805
Gt. Britain
(011) 44-12-8357-5671

This resort is located not far from historic Litchfield, tucked away in the rolling countryside of Staffordshire. It was built in 1860 as a wedding gift to Lady Emily Charlotte, the daughter of Viscount Halifax, from her husband, Hoar Cross Hall, and has been restored to its original beauty, with a modern health spa added. Bedrooms are exquisitely furnished, many with Jacuzzis and antique four-poster beds.

The revitalization of the body's energy through the use of water-based treatments and physical activity is the basis of this spa's philosophy. Healthy eating is also part of the program in the resort's two superb restaurants where you may choose low-calorie or gourmet cuisine.

FACILITIES—Aerobics, yoga and meditation, golf, tennis, racquet sports, bicycling, weight and cardiovascular equipment, fitness profiles, an indoor pool, body treatments, massage, skin care treatments, a beauty salon, hydrotherapy.

PRICE—$659 to $1,537 for three-night to seven-night packages. The price includes single accommodations, three meals daily, a pool, a whirlpool, heat treatments, steam and sauna, exercise classes, a variety of skin and body treatments, including hydrotherapy, and a mini-fitness profile.

Hotel Terme Di Saturnia
58050 Saturnia
Grosseto, Italy
(011) 39-0564-60011

The benefits of this tranquil area between Rome and Florence have been celebrated since the ancient days of Pliny and Titus Livius. Today, the Hotel Terme Di Saturnia overlooks a lake of sulphur-rich thermal waters. The thermal waters have been used for healing purposes through the centuries, and today Terme di Saturnia's line of skin care and beauty products is famous throughout the world. Accommodations are in a luxurious villa set against some of Italy's most lush scenery.

FACILITIES—Diagnostic and skin care treatments, body treatments, massage, hydrotherapy, golf, tennis, horseback riding, bicycling, weight and cardiovascular equipment, fitness profiles, an outdoor pool.

PRICE—$1,468 to $2,092 for various types of seven-night packages. The price includes single accommodations, three meals daily, a medical checkup, a variety of skin and body treatments according to the package, use of the facilities, including a thermal spa and sauna, tennis.

Personal Commentary

One of the authors had the pleasure of a week's stay at two of the spas described in this chapter, the Rancho La Puerto in Baja California, Mexico and the Red Mountain Spa in Ivins, Utah. Fantastic! That is the best word to describe each stay. Each spa provided what they promise and much more. The food is low calorie and delicious, proving you can enjoy what you eat and still not pile on the pounds. In fact, the author lost a few pounds at both spas. The wide range of facilities at each spa allows for individual taste, so there is something for everyone. The staff is knowledgeable and friendly. One leaves these spas feeling refreshed and revitalized. There is also a sense of well-being and renewal. And with all the beauty treatments the author enjoyed, she couldn't help but feel younger, prettier, and even radiant.

We hope we have whetted your appetite to try one of these excellent spas. Most often you'll come away from a spa vacation with life-changing skills to become healthier, more fit, and relaxed. You'll feel the burden of stress being lifted from your shoulders. No doubt your face will be glowing and your body a bit firmer and a few pounds lighter. Most of all you'll come away with the knowledge and skills that help keep you that way. What more can anyone ask of a vacation—your mind, body, and spirit deserve nothing less!

——— 12 ———

Life on the High Seas

One of the gladdest moments of human life is the departure upon a distant journey into unknown lands.—Sir Richard Burton (explorer)

"You haven't lived until you've cruised," said one woman. Is this true? Over six million Americans cruised in 2000, and that figure is projected to grow to well over eight million in the near future. Do you think you're too young for cruising? Or too old? Or that singles don't cruise? Well, forget it! The average age of cruisers has fallen to forty-nine, and the fastest growing cruise population is in the twenty-five to thirty-nine age group. Almost half of current cruise customers are under forty. Most first-timers are even younger, and one-third are single. (If that surprises you, consider that over seventy million Americans are single.)

What makes a cruise vacation different from a resort vacation? The mysterious, beautiful ocean makes all the difference. And resorts stay in one place, while cruise ships take you to spectacular islands and exotic cities, all over the world. A cruise ship is a floating resort, a utopia at sea. Your typical cruise consists of bountiful food, unlimited activities, deep relaxation, and wall-to-wall fun. It is a place where you don't have to make any decisions because everything is planned for you. You need never be alone, because thousands of cruisers sail right along with you. And you don't have to worry about packing and repacking, checking in and out of hotels, land transportation, flights, or any kind of schedule whatsoever. There are lots of activities on the ship and plenty to see and do when you get off at ports (the average one-week cruise visits four). You can spend the entire day exploring new territory or you can just stay put aboard the ship and enjoy its facilities. We guarantee you will never be bored.

Cruises can be economical too, especially if you follow our advice and get one at a good price (see the "Money-Saving Tips" section at the end of this chapter). You won't overspend on your vacation because practically every expense is included in your fare, including your room, meals, entertainment, and, in most cases, air-fare as well. Thus, you eliminate the extra expenses that normally crop up on other vacations (the exception being the cost of the onshore tours, which can run upward of $20 a day.) The cost of a cruise runs from $599 per person (plus tips) for a seven-day trip, available on some of the most popular mass-market lines, to $5,000 on the ultraluxury Silversea, rated the world's best cruise line. Cost is determined by what line you choose, how exotic the destination is, length of time, and your choice of accommodations, which vary greatly. You can book the lowest-priced inside cabin with no port-hole, an outside cabin (with a window), bunk beds or twin beds for roommates, or a luxurious suite. Some cabins come with a veranda on which you can dine as you watch the sunset. Regardless of what cabin you book, you get a private bathroom, a shower, possibly a bathtub, and one or two closets. The rooms are usually modern and nicely furnished, and come with TV and radio. Some lines offer larger cabins for the same price.

By the way, make sure you ask in advance about the size of the cabins and the configuration. Regardless of the size of the ship, make sure that your cabin is situated so that there is no equip-ment or lifeboats blocking the scenery. You may not be able to see this in the ship's diagram, because many do not specify which cabins have a partial or blocked view. Ask the line directly or have your travel agent find out exactly what you will see from your port-hole. And if you are a very allergic person, you might want to stick to a smoke-free ship. Carnival Cruises has them; ask the other lines about this when you book.

One thing you should know is that the prices that are quoted to you are what you will pay per person if two people are sharing a room (double occupancy). If you are traveling alone, and don't want the cruise line to fix you up with a roommate, you may have to pay two fares for the one room. Try to choose a cruise line that has a single supplement, which typically means you pay an additional 50 percent over the per person/double occupancy rate; otherwise you may have to pay double the rate. To get fixed up with a roommate, ask your travel agent to suggest lines that have what are called "share programs." Not only might you gain a new friend, but you will also pay just the regular double-occupancy rate for one person. Keep in mind that some cabins have bunk beds. If you can't climb a ladder, make sure you discuss this with your potential cabinmate.

Meanwhile, if you want to be assured of *male*, not just female, companionship, make sure you book a line that has "social" or "gentlemen" hosts. These attractive and distinguished single men, typically retired professionals in their forties, fifties, and sixties (or older), are hired by the cruise line to dance and socialize with the passengers. Lines that have them include: American Hawaii, Holland America, Cunard, Crystal, Delta Queen, Orient, Royal Olympic, Silversea, and World Explorer. These hosts are personable, affable men who are good dancers. They have been known to date and subsequently marry some of their passenger-guests, after their tour of duty is over (no real dating is allowed on board).

If you're really determined to find romance on your cruise, check with Windjammer Barefoot Cruises. It offers singles-only cruises several times a year. Also try Single World in Rye, New York at (800) 223-6490 or Golden Age Travelers in San Francisco, California at (800) 258-8880. Two newsletters offer advice for those sailing solo. *Travel Companion* in Amityville, New York, at (800) 392-1256 and The *Single Traveler* in Northbrook, Illinois, at

(708) 272-6788. *MaidenVoyages* is a magazine published in San Francisco for women travelers, at (800) 528-8425.

Cruise Issues to Consider

Before you book anything, there are a number of issues to consider and decisions to be made based on your personality, taste, style, and preferences. It's important to think about exactly what will make you happy on a cruise and what might actually make you miserable.

Destination/Theme

First, let's talk about destinations. Where would you be happiest sailing? Europe? Alaska? Africa? Would the Caribbean suit you? Mexico? The Greek Islands? Asian ports? How would you like a riverboat cruise up the Amazon, an icebreaker to the Antarctic, or a cruise to see wildlife in the Galapagos Islands? When thinking about where to go, keep in mind that faraway ports are usually less crowded, and you will be able to take in the sights without being jostled by other passengers. Faraway ports also tend to be longer trips that are more expensive, and these attract an older crowd—which might be just what you want. Closer destinations, such as the Caribbean, attract younger crowds and are actually becoming quite overcrowded.

Do you want intellectually stimulating vacations, full of museums and historic sights? Europe, for example, has a coastline that runs over 24,000 miles and has historic sights practically all along the way. You could also sail to such remote destinations as Zanzibar, the Sea of Cortex, Bora Bora, Bali, Fiji, Patagonia, the Northwest Passage, the Yangtze. From New England to New Zealand, from South America to the South Pacific, from the Mediterranean to the South China Sea. There are over 1,800 ports visited by cruise ships and that figure continues to rise.

Maybe the destination isn't as important to you as what you do on the cruise. If you have a very strong interest or hobby, perhaps you'd like a "special interest" cruise. Just about all the lines offer a variety of theme cruises, and they seem to cover anything you can think of: hobbies, dance, food, classical music, wine, financial planning, murder mysteries—you name it and there's a theme cruise for it. If you do pick a cruise like this, make sure that you have a true interest in the subject, since it is the major activity on the cruise.

Type and Size of Ship

Cruise ships come in small, medium, and large, and there are advantages (and disadvantages) to each. If you want entertainment and resortlike facilities, look for a megaship to satisfy your desires. *Explorer of the Seas* and her sister ship *Voyager of the Seas* (Royal Caribbean), for example, are reputed to be the two largest ships in the world and each carries more than 3,000 passengers. Among the amenities they offer are a Rollerblade track, miniature golf, a rock climbing wall, an ice rink, and a helipad. The *Grand Princess* (Princess Cruises) has a wedding chapel (you never know), five pools, three theaters, and twenty-four-hour dining. Celebrity's *Galaxy* has an ultramodern spa with three levels of pampering; but you should know that it costs extra, starting at $200 per day for the lowest level.

A megaship might be right for you if you would answer "yes" to all of the following questions:

- Do you enjoy glitz and glamour? Megaships are crowded, noisy, and festive, and people typically dress to the nines for dinner.
- Do you crave resort-style amenities, such as Olympic-size pools, miniature golf, tennis courts, and large-screen movie theaters? You'll get all that and more.
- Are you likely to get bored on a ship with minimal entertainment? Megaships have full-scale lounges, bars, and night-

clubs, which may make it easier for you to meet other
people.
- Do you feel comfortable in big crowds? The large cruise
ships hold over 3,000 people.
- Are you prone to motion sickness? The bigger the ship, the
less motion you feel.

On the other hand, if being among thousands of other passengers would make you uncomfortable, you may be happier on a
smaller ship. The smallest cruise ships could have as few as seventy-five people (and a freighter might have as few as ten). It's
easier to make friends because you probably see the same people
every day, on the tours and in the evening at dinner. You might
even get to know the crew. The atmosphere on a smaller ship
tends to be more low-key. Also, smaller ships are able to go to
more destinations. The megaships, some of which are the size of
several city blocks, can't dock in every port and therefore go to
fewer places.

Keep in mind that your choice of a destination may determine
the ship's size. The megaships usually ply the waters of Alaska, the
Caribbean, and Mexico. The smaller ones tend to sail the coasts of
Europe and Asia, offering cruises of ten, twelve, or more days.
The real small ships, which are often referred to as private yachts,
tend to go to more out-of-the-way ports all over the world.

Other Considerations

Here are some other questions you should ask yourself to help
you choose the right cruise:

- When is the best *time* for you to get away? Keep in mind
that more singles go cruising in the summertime.
- How long a trip will you take? Consider that, in general,
older singles tend to take the longer cruises.

- Is the quality of the food very important to you? Most lines have excellent food, but the ultra luxurious lines will offer the height of gourmet.
- Do you like structured onshore tours? If you want guided tours, be sure to get a schedule of tours before your trip, and be prepared to reserve the ones you want your first night on the ship; the best tours fill up quickly.
- What type and age of people are you comfortable with? Remember, the more economical the cruise, the more diversified the passenger list will be, from seniors to college students, from honeymooners to middle-aged couples. The more expensive the cruise, the older the passengers will tend to be.
- Do you tend to become unnerved by too much glitz and formality? You might want to consider a Windjammer Barefoot cruise on a real sailing vessel, a river barge, a freighter, or World Explorer's Alaska cruise, which all provide a very casual atmosphere.
- Do you want a new ship or do you prefer the sense of tradition that comes with an older one?
- How important is it that a doctor be available to you? There are usually doctors aboard all ships, but if you have any medical problems—or doubts—check this out first.

Special Information for Lesbian Travelers

Are you looking for a cruise designed particularly for lesbian travelers? Check with these agencies to learn what voyages are being offered for the lesbian traveler.

Alyson Adventures
PO Box 181223
Boston, MA 02118
(617) 247-8170
or 800-825-9766.

Empress Travel
(800) 429-6969

Olivia Travel
(800) 631-6277

Pied Piper Travel
330 West 42nd Street
New York, NY 10036
(212) 239-2412; outside New York
(800) 874-7312

RSVP Travel Productions
2800 University Avenue, S.E.
Minneapolis, MN 55414
(800) 328-7787 or (612) 379-4697

The Cruise Lines

Now that you have a better idea of what would make your cruise vacation meet all your needs, let's take a closer look at some of America's most popular cruise lines.

American Hawaii Cruises & United States Line
1380 Port of New Orleans Pl.
New Orleans, LA 70130
(800) 765-7000 for American Hawaii;
www.cruisehawaii.com
(877) 330-6600 for United States Line;
www.unitedstateslines.com

DESTINATIONS—Both lines leave from Hawaii and are owned by American Classic Voyages. American Hawaii Cruises has one ship, the SS *Independence*, which sails around the Hawaiian Islands on seven-day cruises, departing from the island of Maui. The *Independence* holds 1,063 passengers. The United States Lines has the MS *Patriot*, which leaves from Honolulu, for a seven-day cruise as well. It sails to the same ports, and can hold 1,212 passengers.

SINGLES ACCOMMODATIONS—The *Independence* has twenty single-occupancy cabins (with one bed) that you can book for usually half the rate of the regular double-occupancy fare. These cabins go quickly and thus may not be available when you book. Single supplements, which range from 33 percent to 100 percent more, are charged for a double-occupancy cabin occupied by one person. The MS *Patriot* does not have single-occupancy cabins.

WHEN TO GO—Since Hawaii is a year-round destination, you might want to consider going during the off-season when you will find fewer families and children. While there is no official off-season, May and September seem a little less busy than the other months. In general, avoid going during the Christmas, New Year, and Easter vacations. The holidays, particularly Easter, tend to be very popular for family groups.

Carnival Cruise Lines
3655 N.W. 87th Ave.
Miami, FL 33178
(305) 599-2600 or (800) 227-6482
www.carnival.com

DESTINATIONS—The Carnival fleet includes superliners and mega-liners as well as traditional ships, and they cruise year-round to the Bahamas, Caribbean, and the U.S. West Coast/Mexican Rivera. These destinations are the mainstays of its cruise packages, and voyages usually take seven days or less. If you have limited time and tend to take shorter, more frequent vacations rather than the traditional one-week or two-week vacation, check out Carnival. Sailing out of Los Angeles, some Carnival ships cruise the Pacific coast of Mexico. There is also a four-day sail to Cozumel in Mexico, leaving either from Tampa or Miami. Carnival also sails to Alaska in the summer, through the Panama Canal, and to Hawaii.

SINGLE ACCOMMODATION—Carnival Cruise Lines especially welcomes singles, and is the line generally most associated with the singles crowd. Singles aged fifty and over are eligible for Carnival's expanded discount. To qualify, singles must be members of the American Association of Retired Persons (AARP). Carnival offers a share program, in which singles are matched with same-sex roommates, according to age and attitude about smoking. We suggest you try the program; it's a good deal.

WHEN TO GO—Springtime is the most popular season for young singles, because of college vacations. During the summer, you will find a good mix of ages. More children will be on board then, but there is still a broad mix. Summer is the most expensive time to cruise, because it's considered high season, when everyone takes a vacation. Winter is also high season, but not as high as summer. Fall is the most value-oriented time to cruise, and there should be a broad mix of passengers then as well.

Celebrity Cruises
1050 Caribbean Way
Miami, FL 331321
(305) 539-6000 or (800) 437-3111
www.celebrity-cruises.com

DESTINATIONS—Celebrity offers cruises from seven to sixteen nights, sailing to the Caribbean, Bermuda, Alaska, Panama Canal, and with coastal and South American itineraries. Celebrity also does the New York-to-Bermuda run.

SINGLES ACCOMMODATIONS—Celebrity does not offer a singles share program and does not have single cabins. Therefore if you plan to sail by yourself, you will have to pay double the fare and stay in a double-occupancy cabin. On the longer, more expensive trips, like the Panama Canal, you may have to pay only 50 percent more.

Clipper Cruise Line
7711 Bonhomme Ave.
St Louis, MO 63105
(314) 727-2929 or (800) 325-0010
www.clippercruise.com

DESTINATIONS—Clipper Cruise Line sails four small ships that are like private yachts and have unusual itineraries. You can sail from Greenland to the Northwest Passage on the line's expedition to the Top of the World. Alternatively, you can look into its series of adventure cruises with itineraries in Indonesia, Australia's Great Barrier Reef, New Zealand, China, Japan, and the islands of the North Pacific. The ships' small size often allows them into areas not accessible to big cruise ships, so you can cruise the hidden fjords of Alaska, serene Caribbean coves, the Amazon rivers in South America, as well as the small Mediterranean islands, or the ice-scapes of Antarctica.

SINGLES ACCOMMODATIONS—The line frequently pairs up people who are looking for roommates. The single supplement is 50 percent more for a "category two" cabin (the only category offered for this rate). If this category is not available they may offer an upgraded cabin for the same rate. It's a good idea to talk to Clipper's reservation people and see what they can do. From time to time they offer a non-advertised discount to a new client. The line occasionally offers discounts to groups, such as the Smithsonian or National Geographic Society.

WHEN TO GO—Seventy percent of Clipper's passengers are repeaters, and their small ships only hold anywhere from 102 to 138 passengers, so it doesn't really have a slow season.

Costa Cruises
80 Southwest Eighth St.
Miami, FL 33130
(305) 375-0676 or (800) 332-6782
www.costacruises.com

DESTINATIONS—Costa Cruise Lines is known for its romantic ships (*Costa Romantica*) and distinct Italian flavor. Costa is also the leading cruise line in Europe, and its seven luxurious ships cruise the world. Costa offers 214 sailings to ninety-five different ports, forty-six different itineraries to forty-two countries including Europe and the United States.

SINGLE ACCOMMODATIONS—Costa does not specifically target singles as some other lines do, but they do have a lot of single cruisers who do not necessarily travel alone. Costa does not offer a singles' share program. Singles can stay alone in a cabin but must pay 150 percent or 200 percent of the rate, depending upon the ship and the sailing. The line does offer a special *"andiamo"* rate for older travelers (sixty and up), if you book early. And you can even get $100 off the special *andiamo* fare, which is per cabin, double occupancy, but only for Caribbean bookings. There are other discounts available for two people in a cabin ranging from $1,100 off per cabin for the Caribbean to $1,600 off per cabin for a European cruise. Check with your travel agent for sailings and dates.

WHEN TO GO—Costa deploys all of its vessels to Europe for the high season, and its entire fleet is there from May to October. Costa has two ships in the United States in the Caribbean from November to April.

Holland America
300 Elliott Ave. W.
Seattle, WA 98119
(877) 724-5425
www.hollandamerica.com

DESTINATIONS—Holland America has been in business for over 127 years, making it one of the oldest cruise lines around. You can sail on Holland America to 253 destinations worldwide, including Alaska, the Caribbean, Panama Canal, Hawaii, the Mexican Riviera and Pacific Coast, Eastern Canada and New England, Europe, the western and eastern Mediterranean, and South America. It also offers a Grand World Voyage, the ultimate vacation, which is a cruise around the world. This is a ninety-nine-day cruise, which the line has been doing for almost thirty-five years. You can elect to merely take various segments of this spectacular cruise, featuring the attractions of major world cities coupled with rare adventures in thirty-seven ports on six continents around the globe. One of the beauties of the world cruise is that you can get on at any place and get off at any subsequent point. It provides the opportunity for a cruise from about ten days up to almost one hundred days, and this is priced according to the segment you pick. If you want the entire world cruise, prices run from $20,000 to $160,000 depending upon accommodations.

The line also offers up to twenty theme cruises with eleven different topics, including Greats of Broadway, Dixieland Jazz, A Tribute to Sinatra, Big Band sound, Sock Hop (rock-and-roll oldies), Country Western, and Bingo, among others. These run from twelve to sixteen days.

Another favorite on Holland America is the University at Sea program, which offers courses on topics such as computers and continuing education on surgery (mostly for doctors). This is a paid program offered on many ships, and fees may range anywhere from $200 to $600 depending upon the course, many of which offer official credits.

SINGLES ACCOMMODATIONS—Holland America has a share program if you want a roommate. They will guarantee the share, but you won't initally always know what cabin you will be assigned. The line sets aside a certain number of cabins on each of their sailings for this program, and they will match you by gender, age, and smoking preferences. If no roommate is available in the category you request in the share program, they may bump you up into a better cabin category where a roommate exists at no extra charge to you. If they can't find you a roommate you will still sail in the cabin for the same price. If you request a category that is not in the share program or you absolutely want a room by yourself, you pay 150 percent more for a standard outside double cabin and 200 percent for a penthouse. Holland America recommends that you book as early as possible for this program. But if you do book early, be sure to tell your travel agent that if a better rate for the cruise you've selected becomes available, you want to get it. Keep checking the newspapers and travel ads after you've booked.

WHEN TO GO—Holland America says this depends upon where you want to go. If the season doesn't matter to you, the destination might. South America and New England cruises sell out early. May in Europe is less crowded but the most congested month is July. August is the busiest time in Alaska. January and February are very busy in the Caribbean. If you are looking for the line's social hosts check cruises of ten days or longer, and always ask your travel agent about them.

Norwegian Cruise Line
7665 Corporate Center Dr.
Miami, FL 33126
(305) 436-0866 or (800) 327-7030
www.ncl.com

DESTINATIONS—This line is known for its fabulous entertainment and its acclaimed sports and special-interest cruises. Their six superliners sail to the Bahamas and Caribbean year-round (except for September and October), and the Panama Canal in April and November (check for repositioning bargains). From spring to fall, cruises go to Bermuda and Alaska. They also offer a series of Mediterranean sailings.

SINGLES ACCOMMODATIONS—Norwegian does not have a share program, but it does offer what they call a *guaranteed single rate* on selected sailings. The line will guarantee the sailing and the date, but it will not guarantee which cabin you will stay in, and it will make the cabin selection for you. This offer, however, is available only on selected sailings, and you have to check with the line or your travel agent to see which ones have it. You can save up to 50 percent this way (savings based upon picking your own cabin). However, if you definitely want to select your own cabin, depending upon availability, you might have to pay 150 to 200 percent of the usual fare.

Princess Cruises
10100 Santa Monica Blvd.
Suite 1800
Los Angeles, CA 90067
(310) 553-1770 or (800)774-6237
www.princess.com

DESTINATIONS—Princess Cruises is one of the three largest cruise lines in the industry, operating a fleet of nine ships that call at over 220 ports worldwide. Princess offers cruises to more than 150 different destinations.

SINGLES ACCOMMODATIONS—Princess does have a singles share program that will match you up with another single woman. It is offered on all ships but only for certain cabin categories, and those categories will vary by ship. On the *Grand Princess, Sun Princess, Dawn Princess, Sea Princess, Ocean Princess, Regal Princess* and *Crown Princess,* it is available with one outside and two inside categories of staterooms. On the *Royal Princess* and *Pacific Princess,* it is available with one outside and one inside category of staterooms. All share program participants are matched with same-sex cabin mates. If there is no match for you, you will not have to pay a supplemental fee as a "single" passenger, and will be assigned a stateroom to yourself in the category booked. The share program is not included in any special national or regional promotional fares offered during the year. The only other special rates available is the "Love Boat Savers" fares, for those who book early. If you decide to go alone, without a cabin mate, you will pay anywhere from 150 percent to 200 percent of the standard fare, depending upon the cabin category booked. Women traveling this way can book any type of cabin.

WHEN TO GO—You may find more younger singles in the summer. If the season is immaterial to you, then go in the fall when you might find some good discounts. Older singles travel year-round on cruises of ten days or more to exotic places.

Royal Caribbean International
1050 Caribbean Way
Miami, FL 33132
(800) 327-6700
www.royalcaribbean.com

DESTINATIONS—One of the largest cruise lines in the world, Royal Caribbean has thirteen modern ships and offers sixty-six different itineraries that include a total of 160 destinations, including Alaska, the Bahamas, Bermuda, the Caribbean, Europe, Southeast Asia and the Far East, Hawaii, Mexico, Panama Canal, Russia, and Scandinavia. They also offer a short cruise of four days from Miami to the Bahamas that is very popular with younger singles. Other trips popular with singles are the four-night cruises out of Los Angeles to Encinitas and San Diego, the seven-night Caribbean cruises, and the seven-night cruise from New York to Bermuda. Royal Caribbean has the two largest ships in the world, the *Explorer of the Seas* and the *Voyager of the Seas* (sister ships). If you want to experience these mammoth virtual floating resorts at sea and all that they offer, ask your travel agent to specifically book you on either one.

SINGLES ACCOMMODATIONS—Royal Caribbean does not have a share program for singles, and if you want your own cabin you will have to pay the full rate that two people would pay for the double occupancy of the room.

Windjammer Barefoot Cruises
1759 Bay Road
Miami, FL 33139
(800) 327-2601
www.windjammer.com

DESTINATIONS—Windjammer has the largest fleet of privately owned, small sailing vessels. It tries to place each of its six ships in the area best suited to it. The itineraries are very diverse, including relatively isolated beach destinations and uninhabited islands with some of the best diving and snorkeling.

SINGLES ACCOMMODATIONS—Windjammer will try to find you a roommate, and if they can't, you will not have to pay any additional charge to stay alone in a cabin. They match for gender only, not age; smoking is not allowed in any of the cabins. You do not find out what your roommate status is until the manifest is prepared or around boarding time, but you can be sure you will stay in a standard cabin, since the other type of cabin only has double beds and thus is not available for shares. The standard cabin comes with an upper and lower bed, and the lower bed is usually a wider one. If a woman wants a single cabin she will have to pay 75 percent more, but if it is a holiday sailing like Christmas or the New Year, or high season (February/March) it will be the full room rate that two people would pay (100 percent more). Some ships have single occupancy, others only have double occupancy. Remember these are small sailing ships that carry between sixty-four and 122 passengers.

WHEN TO GO—Windjammer's high season is whenever it is cold up north, and they usually have more requests than they can handle on some of their ships. In the winter they have more couples; in the summer more singles. There are also "singles-only" cruises six to ten times a year, and the line is strict in maintaining a balanced booking of men and women. The age range is twenty to sixty, with thirty-five to forty-five being the largest group. These cruises are extremely popular with repeaters. Windjammer recently started theme cruises that include a golf cruise, taste-of-the island cruise, spirits of the Caribbean cruise, bird-watching and botanical island cruise, photography cruise, paint-the-island cruise, and a "sea of wellness" cruise.

Ultra Luxury Cruise Lines

If you are looking for the finest in luxury, gourmet food, and lavish cabins and suites, check out some of these lines. Their rates, many of which include liquor and tips, are much higher than the mass-market cruises listed in the first section, but you can frequently find bargains when they reposition their ships. They also run special pricing from time to time. Your travel agent can help you in your selection.

Crystal Cruises
2049 Century Park East,
Suite 1400
Los Angeles, CA 90067
(310) 785-9300 or (800) 820-6663
www.crystalcruises.com

Raddison Seven Seas Cruises
600 Corporate Drive, Suite 410
Fort Lauderdale, FL 33334
(800) 285-1835
www.rssc.com

Seabourn Cruise Line
6100 Blue Lagoon Drive,
Suite 400

Miami, FL 33126
(800) 929-9391
www.seabourn.com

Silversea Cruises
110 East Broward Boulevard
Fort Lauderdale, FL 33301
(954) 522-2299
or (800) 722-9955
www.silversea.com

Windstar Cruises
300 Elliott Avenue West
Seattle, WA 98119
(877) 827-7245
www.windstarcruises.com

Money-Saving Tips

When you finally make that big decision to sail, you will face an even bigger decision: how to go about finding the best deal. Some say you should wait for the last moment, others say you should book well in advance to get an early-bird discount. Who offers true value and how can you tell the difference? We hope the following tips will give you some insight into the dizzying world of discounts, price slashings, best bargains, and travel clubs. That way you can always be sure to get the best deal.

- **Book early.** People who book early, anywhere from six months or less from the sailing date may be rewarded with both the lowest price and the best choice of cabins. Most of the reputable cruise brokers or cruise discounters offer what's called price protection: If the cruise line drops its price after you book, the broker will reduce the price to the new lower price, as long as the cruise line will pass the lower price onto the broker, which they will almost always do.

- **Ask about share programs.** Many lines offer share programs, matching for sex, age, and smoking. By getting a roommate, you pay the standard per person rate for a double-occupancy cabin, rather than paying 50 percent to 100 percent more to stay alone. And if a roommate can't be found, some cruise lines will give you that lower rate anyway, and you will have the cabin to yourself. Be sure to ask your travel agent if the cruise line you want to sail on has a share program.

- **Look for seasonal bargains.** These cruises are the best-kept secrets in the cruise industry. Seasonal bargains vary according to destination. If you plan to go to the Caribbean, the fall would have the best bargains. If you want Alaska, September and October will be cheaper. If you're talking about Europe, it really depends more on the availability of a special offer. Ask your agent about this.

- **Ask about repositioning cruises.** In the spring and fall, some of the ships leave their regular cruise itineraries and reposition themselves to other areas. For example, every fall, ships reposition themselves from Alaska, Europe, New York, and many exotic regions to the warm-weather areas for winter cruising. There are great deals to be found when this happens. Cruise lines that have longer routes (and are therefore much more expensive) usually offer these repositioning cruises. Ships in Alaska move down the coast, through the Panama Canal. Ships in the Mediterranean cross the Atlantic to get to the Caribbean. Many lines will offer a two-for-one deal on repositioning cruises, and passengers are often upgraded to cabins better than the ones they selected. Ask your agent about them.

- **Think about freighters.** If you want to travel the world on a budget, think about a freighter. People who travel this way are older, many retired. Many freighters offer amenities and luxuries not previously found, and you will meet a hardy breed of cruiser. The number of passengers is very limited on freighters, and many will carry no more than twelve people, which is the limit for sailing without a full-time physician. The cabins are not as luxurious as you would find on a regular cruise ship, but they will be air-conditioned and have a private bath. Some even offer minibars and refrigerators and rooms with a view. You will normally eat with fellow passengers in a separate dining room, and many have a swimming pool, TV lounge, exercise room, and sauna. These facilities are usually shared with the ship's officers.

  For example, the 45,000-ton *Hong Kong Senator*, a German-flag container ship built in 1993, will take ten passengers. It makes a roundtrip of fifty-six days, leaving from San Francisco, then sailing to Mexico, through the Panama Canal, and on to Georgia, Virginia, and New York. It then crosses the Atlantic to Europe. It comes back by way of New York and ends up in Los Angeles. Fares start at $3,640 per person in double occupancy.

  The time spent in any particular port is determined by the time spent loading and unloading freight. However, you usually have a longer time for sight-seeing than if you were on a cruise ship. Years ago you could get a number of freighters to sail on; unfortunately many have stopped taking on passengers. Some companies and travel clubs that still offer freighter cruises include:

**Compagnie Polynesienne
De Transport Maritime**
2028 El Camino Real South,
Suite B
San Mateo, CA 94403

(650) 574-2575 or (800) 972-7268;
fax (650) 574-6881
www.aranui.com
(service from Tahiti to the
Marquesas Islands)

Curnow Shipping
c/o Golden Bear Travel
16 Digital Drive
Novato, CA 94949
(415) 382-8900 or (800) 551-1000;
fax (415) 382-9086.

Maris Freighter Cruises
215 Main Street
Westport, CN 06880
(203) 222-1500 or (800) 996-2747;
fax (203) 222-9191
www.freightercruises.com

Freighter World Cruises
180 South Lake Avenue,
Suite 335
Pasadena, CA 91101
(626) 449-3106 or (800) 531-7774;
fax (626) 449-9573
www.freighterworld.com

Travltips Cruise And Freighter Travel Association
P.O. Box 580188
Flushing, NY 11358
(718) 939-2400
fax (718) 939-2047
www.travltips.com

Freighter Travel Club of America
3524 Harts Lake Road
Roy, WA 98580
(360) 458-4178

- **Check out the discounters.** You may find substantial discounts here, so check them before booking.

  Spur of the Moment Tours & Cruises (800) 343-1991.
  The Cruise Line Inc. (800) 777-0707.
  Moment's Notice (718) 234-6295.
  National Discount Cruise Co. (800) 788-8108.
  Short Notice Vacations Savings Card (800) 444-9800.
  Vacations to Go (800) 338-4962.
  World Wide Cruises (800) 882-9000.
  Worldwide Discount Travel Club (800) 446-9938.
  Cruise Only (800) 209-9871.
  The Cruise People (800) 892-7630.
  Discount Cruise Brokers (800) 682-5122.

Another thing to take into consideration when budgeting for a cruise is the cost of tipping. Many of the lines say they have a "no tipping" policy or that "no tipping is required." However, the ship's staff still expect tips and do deserve them, regardless of what the lines state. Talk to your travel agent and find out how much tipping will add to the cost of your trip.

Conclusion

Certainly one of the highest of highs is that feeling of anticipation when a new journey lies ahead of us. It is at those precise times, contemplating all the sights, sounds, and wonders of a new location our feet have never before traveled, when there are all the possibilities of new people and places just before us, that we say: It just doesn't get any better than this!

Yes, there are decisions to make when planning a trip to unknown territories, and there are chores to do before you go, and it may be a little scary to venture out solo, but there's nothing to equal the feeling of excitement and anticipation when you finally pack your bag, lock your door, and set upon an adventure that will introduce you to another phenomenal place on our planet.

Hopefully, now that you have come to the final chapter of this book it will have opened your mind and heart to take advantage of all of the travel opportunities just waiting to make your dreams come true. Remember, it is up to you to travel the paths that will fill your life with never-to-be-forgotten journeys.

Index

189